The Outboard Book

by Nigel Warren

Motor Boating & Sailing Books

Acknowledgements

Many of the test results given in this book have been published over a number of years in the magazine *Practical Boat Owner*. These tests were mostly contrived between *PBO* and E P Barrus Ltd, the importers of Johnson outboards. E P Barrus have also helped otherwise during the preparation of this book. Other *PBO* tests have included Chrysler, Mercury, Yamaha and Warrenjet. Other test results in the book have been extracted from highly detailed reports in *Neptune Nautisme*. Beryl Riches did the drawings.

Published by Motor Boating & Sailing Books
224 West 57th Street
New York, New York 10019

Editor's Prologue

Motor Boating & Sailing is proud to be able to give American outboard owners and prospective owners a chance to avail themselves of Nigel Warren's excellent book.

We reviewed a number of treatments of outboard engines before choosing *The Outboard Book*, and we found Nigel's approach to have just the right mix of authoritative theory and practical advice. There are a great many boatmen who use outboards and for a diversity of purposes; Mr. Warren does admirably well in addressing the entire spectrum.

Since its inception in 1907, *Motor Boating & Sailing* has championed the cause of outboard engines. Our first editor, Charles F. Chapman, raced outboards himself and was devoted to encouraging their widespread use. Today there are millions of outboard owners, a testament to the fact that outboards are still one of the best recreational buys around.

We think this book will do more than its share to help outboard owners understand their engines, their boats, the need for boating safety, and increase their enjoyment of outboard boating.

Jeff Hammond, Editor

Table of Contents

Introduction

Where there is a straight choice between inboard and out-board power, the following factors are involved. An outboard is around half the weight of a gasoline inboard and a quarter of the weight of a diesel inboard of equivalent horsepower, which is a very important aspect on a planing boat. Furthermore, a new outboard is far cheaper than a new diesel inboard, especially when installation costs are added to engine cost. Many gasoline inboards are comparable in price until one takes into account installation costs. With any inboard engine there are items such as mounts, battery, fuel tank, exhaust system, cooling system and through-hull fittings, quite apart from the shaft and propeller, or outdrive. An outboard takes up less space in the boat and can be taken home fairly easily for storage or maintenance, but this also means that it is open to theft, which is a very real problem. The propeller can be easily reached to disentangle weed, old ropes or plastic sacks, which is a distinct advantage on rivers and shallow lakes.

A normal two-stroke outboard consumes more fuel than a four-stroke gasoline inboard engine, while the fuel is an oil mixture rather than neat. A diesel runs on cheaper fuel, besides consuming a considerably smaller volume for the horsepower produced. The comparative consumptions are:

outboard: 0.8 to 1.3 pints (0.4 to 0.62 L) per hour per horse-power.
four-stroke inboard (gasoline): 0.6 to 0.7 pints (0.28 to 0.34 L) per hour per horsepower.
diesel inboard: 0.5 to 0.54 pints (0.23 to 0.26 L) per hour per horsepower.

These are figures for full-throttle or near full-throttle operation;

1

at slower cruising speeds the consumption gap between outboards and inboards widens considerably.

An outboard is necessarily exposed to the elements and there is always the chance of its being swamped at sea. More insidious are the effects of prolonged exposure while the boat is idle: an inboard is naturally more protected. One could also say that an outboard is a less seaworthy proposition than an inboard for seagoing displacement boats, whether power or sail. The exposure factor inherently means less reliability, while in the event of breakdown it is difficult to work on an outboard when the boat is being tossed around in choppy water. For motor boats the installation of two or twin outboards is the answer. A sailing boat has still, of course, its primary source of propulsion, so failure of its outboard is probably more of a nuisance than a disaster, unless the rig is very inefficient. In rough water the boat's pitching tends to disrupt the outboard's thrust more than in the case of an inboard: the outboard's propeller is farther aft (away from the center of pitching) and closer to the surface, besides being smaller. As an auxiliary, an outboard is very much less capable of giving propulsion against strong winds and seas than an inboard of the same nominal horsepower.

Another snag with outboard propulsion, particularly in the case of cabin cruisers, is that steering becomes very vague at low speeds and there is little rudder effect in neutral. On the other hand, when going astern and at planing speeds steering is normally very good. Two-stroke outboards tend to give plug trouble when running slowly for long periods. There is also the electrical power question: an inboard normally has electric starting and a generator, whereas it is usually an extra on outboards. A battery/generator system also allows accessories and lights to be used while the engine is switched off.

Many of the points mentioned so far are discussed more fully in later pages, but it is clear that an outboard is ideal for speedboats and planing cruisers, where its advantages come to the fore and its disadvantages are hardly significant. On the other hand, as an auxiliary on a sailing yacht, or the main power on a displacement motor cruiser, its disadvantages pose several problems.

The development of outboards

The classic outboard motor configuration consists of a two-stroke gasoline engine with a vertical crankshaft driving down via a shaft to bevel gears and hence to the propeller. Reverse is

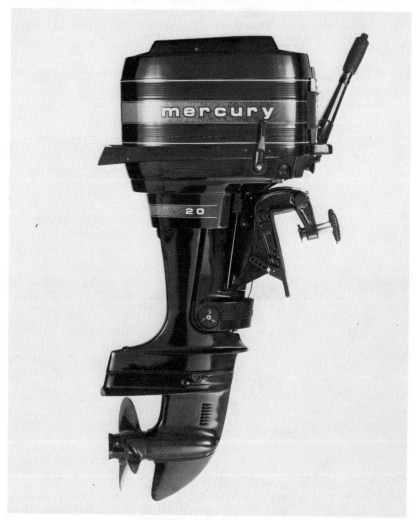

A typical beneficiary of the advanced state of outboard building and design. Such an outboard is incredibly versatile.

achieved in the bevel gears. The engine castings and the leg are usually made of salt water resistant aluminum, for lightness. The motor clamps on to a transom of standard height so that the propeller comes below the bottom of the transom and in a clear flow of water. The clamping arrangement also allows the whole motor to pivot in order to steer the boat, which mean that the thrust of the propeller effects steering, rather than the flow of water over a rudder (as with an inboard installation).

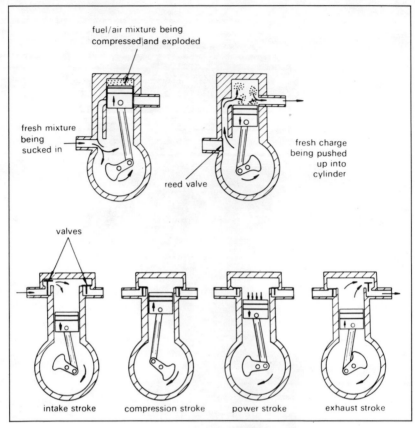

fuel/air mixture being compressed and exploded

fresh mixture being sucked in

reed valve

fresh charge being pushed up into cylinder

valves

intake stroke   compression stroke   power stroke   exhaust stroke

Two-stroke and four-stroke cycles.

The whole motor can also tilt in the fore-and-aft direction in order that the leg can be lifted out of the water when the motor is not in use, or when beaching. Ignition is by magneto, thus making the engine independent of a battery. The fuel tank is a separate item, except on the smallest units where it is fitted on top of the motor.

Why is the two-stroke and not the four-stroke cycle so popular? It makes for a more powerful, lighter and cheaper engine (because there are fewer components). Two-strokes are also smoother running and simpler to maintain. There is a power stroke every time the piston descends the cylinder, whereas in the full-stroke cycle firing occurs at every other revolution of the engine, so theoretically a two-stroke is twice as powerful. But it does mean that there is less time for the cylinder to get rid of the burned gases, and consequently their replacement by fresh fuel/air mixture is not as efficient. This in turn means that rather less than twice the power is developed and the efficiency, and hence the fuel consumption, suffers. A four-stroke has a whole revolution in which to scavenge itself. For the same size cylinder, and therefore for roughly the same size and weight of engine, a two-stroke is more powerful but, per horsepower produced, thirstier.

Compare an outboard engine with a car engine. A 1 liter car engine gives about 40 horsepower at a weight of about 250 pounds (114 kg) excluding the gearbox, whereas a 1 liter outboard gives 70 or 80 hp for a weight, complete, of around 200 pounds (91 kg). One can see the great advantage of the two-stroke where weight is so important, and its bulk is also comparatively small. The modern outboard does not achieve this kind of performance by particularly high revs—5000 to 6000 rpm is normal—nor is its life particularly short. With the number of running hours normal to pleasure craft engines (in the order of 100 per year), an outboard's engine should last as many years as a car. For the owner, the two-stroke motor is simple to maintain; there is no oil sump or filter to change regularly, and no valves to adjust.

The bevel gears at the bottom of the leg reduce the engine's high rpm to a manageable rpm for efficient propeller operation. Usually the propeller revolves at around half the speed of the engine. This ratio is fixed by the gearing, while different sizes of propeller allow an outboard to propel different types of boat. A large heavy boat requires a fine-pitched propeller, otherwise the motor will be overloaded, and a light planing boat requires a coarse-pitched propeller, otherwise the motor will over-rev. Ideally the gear ratio in the hub *and* the propeller size should vary to suit the type of boat: a large, slow-revving propeller (and consequently a large reduction ratio) for slow craft and a smaller, higher-revving propeller for fast ones. A design which enables one to alter the ratio when the motor is taken off one boat and put on another is impractical, so manufacturers choose a compromise ratio and offer a range of propellers.

At planing boat speeds the drag of the lower unit in the water becomes a significant part of the total drag that the propeller has to push against, so the streamlining and correct shaping of this part is very important. At displacement speeds of 5 or 6 knots (9 or 11 km/hr) this drag is insignificant.

Cooling the engine presents a problem, and most outboards are water-cooled. Water is sucked in through a small grill in the lower unit and pumped up and through the water passages of

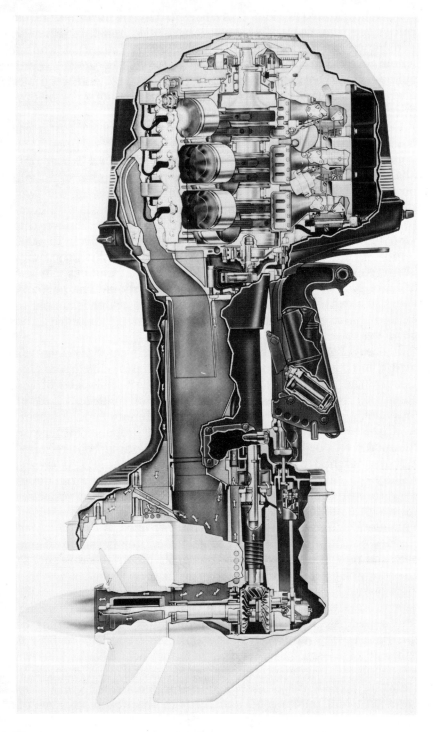

the engine and back out. The alternative is air cooling, but on the larger motors it would be physically impossible to get enough cooling fin area and a sufficient mass flow of air around cylinders producing so much power and waste heat. Air cooling is often adopted for small motors, but generally speaking it produces a noisier engine. On the other hand there is no water pump to fail nor intakes to get blocked. With water cooling a thermostatic control is a desirable feature, especially if the motor is to be usually run at lower revs—trolling, for instance. It keeps the engine temperature higher resulting in better combustion, higher efficiency and less wear.

I have briefly described the typical outboard, but in recent years there have been many technical refinements which have produced significantly better motors, from the owner's point of view, and some of these are worth discussing. For example, the noise and unreliability problems have been tackled. Features which contribute to quietness are an underwater exhaust and a sealed hood over the head. In some motors the exhaust is ejected through the hub of the propeller, which also eliminates the exhaust fume problem. Fiberglass hoods lined on the inside and seated on a rubber gasket confine the noise (mainly mechanical) coming from the engine. Rubber mountings between the clamp bracket and the rest of the outboard not only reduce vibrations reaching the transom of the boat, but in doing so cut down the transmission of noise. Carburetor air intake silencers and an arrangement whereby the exhaust down-pipe is surrounded by cooling water also contribute to noise reduction. Naturally there have been improvements in general engine design and engineering standards which have had an effect on noise levels. Multi-cylinder engines are smoother running than single-cylinder units, and in general are quieter. Even motors of under 10 hp are now often twin-cylinder. Car designers must look upon modern outboard specifications with envy. On many outboards there are separate carburetors for each cylinder in contrast to a single carburetor for four or six cylinders on car engines. Separate carburetors allow higher performance because each cylinder is served with the same amount of fuel/air mixture, besides which the inlet manifolds can be short and straight. Capacitor-discharge (CD) ignition is quite common on outboards, whereas on cars it is rare. Even individual ignition cir-

Arrows indicate the paths of the cooling water. Be sure water is constantly sputtering from the exit nozzle, or the engine will be damaged by overheating.

cuits for each cylinder are sometimes employed.

CD ignition produces a much higher voltage at the spark-plugs, both when starting the engine and when it is running at high rpm. The greater voltage and more instantaneous squirt of electricity mean that the engine is more likely to fire when the plug is cold, oily and coated with carbon. CD ignition also allows the use of surface gap plugs which have a longer life than the ordinary side electrode type. A better spark has slight benefits all round as regards efficient combustion inside the cylinder, so overall engine performance is that much better. Also the all-electric CD system does not have contact breakers, which are a most frequent source of trouble on all engines so fitted, includ-

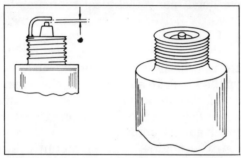

Surface gap sparkplug (right), intended for high voltage CD systems, and an ordinary electrode plug on which the gap should be maintained to the motor maker's specification.

ing car engines. This eliminates the maintenance associated with contact breakers, including checking the timing: with a CD system, once fixed, the timing need never be checked. Altogether, CD ignition is a most worthwhile advance.

Apart from an immense gain in performance, steady research and development has meant increased reliability. A big factor has been ignition waterproofing: totally encapsulated electronic ignition is a big advance. Fixed-jet carburetors ensure that the mixture cannot be inadvertently upset, and perhaps most significantly, the amount of oil in the fuel/oil mixture is now commonly down to 50:1. Pre-war, it was around 8:1, reducing to 25:1 in the 1960s, and this latest development has meant much

This center-console high speed fisherman with her twin outboards can ocean-fish with the big boats, and bring home more than her share of the denizens of the deep.

less carbon formation in the engine, longer-lasting plugs, and less chance of their oiling-up when starting from cold or running slowly. It also means a cleaner exhaust. This low proportion of oil has been achieved largely by improvements in oil performance, and only special outboard oil must be used in engines running on 50:1 mixtures.

Those who go boating in shallow or debris-strewn water with an outboard which has shear-pin protection of the drive gear know how infuriating regular pin changing can be. The introduction of other means of shock-absorbing is a step forward. Many motors now have propellers which are splined on to the shaft, shocks being taken up in a rubber sleeve inserted in the hub.

Facilities for charging a battery for cabin lights, or plugging in navigation lights, and so forth are now available on smaller motors than before. Similarly, electric starting and charging are available for motors of down to 10 hp or so. This is a great boon to fishermen and sailors where large motors and high speeds are definitely not required, but electricity is.

The most important modern technical refinements which give direct benefits from the owners' point of view have been mentioned above, but not particular cylinder scavenging systems— for instance "loop charging." In a two-stroke motor the fuel/air mixture from the carburetor first goes to the crankcase whereupon, as the piston descends on its power stroke, it is com-

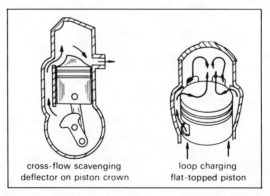

cross-flow scavenging
deflector on piston crown

loop charging
flat-topped piston

Scavenging systems. In loop charging the inlet ports make the jets of fresh charge impinge on each other and flow up and over the domed cylinder head.

pressed and forced, via ports or holes uncovered by the piston, up into the cylinder. By this time the burned gases are already flowing out through other ports in the cylinder walls to the exhaust pipe. In that brief moment before the piston returns up the cylinder they have to be completely expelled from the cylinder and replaced by the fresh mixture. In practice this ideal is not achieved, but if it were, the efficiency of the two-stroke and hence its fuel consumption would then compare with the four-stroke engine. Manufacturers strive to achieve better scavenging of the exhaust gases, and such arrangements as loop charging and direct charging are two examples. It is hard to quantify exactly how much better these systems are, because of the difficulty of comparing like with like. If one tests a 60-hp cross-flow outboard (the older scavenging system) and a 60-hp loop-charged outboard, there may be other differences between the two motors, for instance in cylinder capacity and gear ratio, which may have more effect on the performance and fuel consumption than the difference in scavenging.

However, the following test of two motors tested consecutively on the same boat does show the cumulative effect of modern design. The boat was a 16-foot hard-chine cabin dayboat tested first with the relatively old design 40-hp Johnson and then with the newer 50-hp Johnson. The differences between the two motors are as follows:

	Johnson 40 hp	*Johnson 50 hp*
scavenging system	cross-flow	loop-charged
gear ratio	12:21 (1:75:1)	12:29 (2.42:1)
prop. diam. (in/mm)	10½ (265)	12¼ (310)
cyl. capacity/cc/cu. in.	720 (43.9)	680 (41.5)
ignition	magneto	CD without contact breakers

The modern 50-hp motor gave 5 knots (9.2 km/hr) of extra speed (in about 20 knots) and yet used 0.6 gallons (2.3 L) an hour less fuel in doing so.

Horsepower ratings

When an outboard is said to be of so many horsepower, what is actually meant? Usually it is a truthful statement, but the power figure is usually a "sprint" rating (rather than "continuous") with the motor in tip-top condition, and the horsepower is measured at the crankshaft rather than at the propeller. Due to losses in the bevel gears and bearings, the power at the propeller is in the region of 4 to 12 percent less than at the crankshaft. There is also a very small amount of power absorbed by the water pump.

Most outboards are rated to the BIA (Boating Industry Association) standard, which stipulates that power is measured at the crankshaft at an rpm in the middle of the recommended rev range. The average of five consecutive power readings taken at one minute intervals becomes the certified horsepower rating after correcting to a standard air temperature and pressure. Either two or three standard engines are tested like this, and the average of two taken as the final certified horsepower. The engine must be standard in all details affecting power output; fuel and oil used must be commercially available.

Since a figure arrived at by these means would invariably be anything other than a whole number, the manufacturer can presumably choose to adopt the closest lower whole number or multiple of 5 or 10. On the other hand, outboards rated at 9.9 hp (rather than a round 10) are common, and this is a result of U.S. boating regulations. In fact these engines often produce more than their rated quota.

Manufacturers who do not comply with any recognized horsepower rating often state that their indicated horsepower is equivalent to their competitors'—i.e. their 40-hp motor will give boat performance equivalent to any competitor's 40-hp motor. Consequently, with minor exceptions one can draw the important conclusion that different makes of outboards of the same horsepower are roughly comparable in power, especially in the case of the big makes and their larger motors. Anomalies show up more often on small motors of less than 6 or 8 nominal horsepower.

What's available

The big makes follow the classic or conventional outboard style; they have a large range from the tiniest to the largest motors and vie with each other in producing, year by year, better outboards from a performance point of view. Johnsons and Evinrudes are basically the same, and range in size from 2 hp up to 235 hp. Mercury outboards, in their black livery, range from 2 to 235 hp, and Chrysler motors from 4 to 140 hp. Volvo-Penta and Crescent are Swedish-made motors of basically the same design; all of the range from 4 to 75 hp are loop-scavenged. Yamaha, a Japanese name well known in the motorcycle world, make motors from 2 to 55 hp. Suzuki, another Japanese manufacturer, markets outboards in the U.S. from 2 to 85 hp. Mariner Outboards, a division of Brunswick Corporation's Marine Power

Group, now offers motors from 2 to 175 hp. And Spirit Marine has just begun selling a line of outboards from 2 to 85 hp.

There are a number of other makes of conventional motors which are not so well known outside their country of origin, such as those from Italy, e.g. Selva, Carniti and Ducati. Their respective ranges are 3.5 to 65 hp, 3 to 90 hp, and 5 to 25 hp. Other makes include Tomos from Yugoslavia (3 to 18 hp).

In the under 10 hp class, there are many other makes besides those mentioned so far. Clinton, for example, offers small outboards from 1.5 to 9 hp. Perhaps the best known is the British Seagull, although these motors are really in a class by themselves. They are one design that does not change very much over the years. Old-fashioned in a technical sense and rather noisy, nevertheless they are robust and reliable, and are fitted with large propellers making them almost uniquely suitable for slow-speed propulsion. And there is an excellent direct-from-the-manufacturers (or their agents) cheap spares service. Four models range from $1\frac{1}{2}$ to 5 hp. A rather similar machine is the Whitehead 6 hp from Italy. There is a smooth, quiet 4-hp outboard from Ailsa Craig (a Yugoslavian Tomos engine) that has been popular for some time, and British Anzani with 3- and 5-hp models, and Sea Bee with 2-hp and 4-hp units.

Turning now to unconventional outboards, there are one or two four-strokes. A well-known make is Ocean. They make a 4-hp and an 8-hp, both powered with single-cylinder, air-cooled engines of industrial origin, and are a little noisy and thumpy. Economy in fuel consumption is the main advantage: about half that of a comparable two-stroke at cruising revs. Also, slow running does not cause nearly so much plug fouling or general sooting-up. The fuel is neat gasoline, so there is no mixing with oil to be done.

Another four-stroke outboard is the Honda $7\frac{1}{2}$ hp. I will take this quiet and smooth-running machine as an example for comparison with conventional motors, bearing in mind my earlier remarks about four-strokes. The Honda has a 149 cc (9.1 cu. in.) twin-cylinder, water-cooled, overhead camshaft engine enclosed in a fiberglass hood. The whole outboard weighs 67 pounds (30 kg), which can be compared with the Johnson 6 hp at 51 pounds (23 kg), the Archimedes $7\frac{1}{2}$ hp at 42 pounds (19 kg), or the Mercury $7\frac{1}{2}$ hp at 66 pounds (30 kg). Cost is in the same order as the big makes of equivalent horsepower. A good reduction ratio of 2.75 : 1 is provided, although the engine is quite high-revving (6000 rpm). The main physical distinction of four-stroke outboards is the presence of a sump filled with oil which must be changed regularly as on a car engine. One has to be careful to lay the engine down on one particular side only, otherwise the oil will run out of the filler tube (there is a clear notice to this effect on the hood). From a technical standpoint, it is surprising that this motor is not more popular.

Two- and four-stroke engines can sometimes be converted to run on kerosene, which is a cheaper fuel in many countries. There are one or two outboards designed to run on paraffin, for instance the 15-hp Yamaha. The usual penalties for using this cheaper fuel are loss of power, quicker fouling of the plugs and cylinders, and the necessity of buying and mixing oil with two fuels because the motor has to be started on gasoline mixture and then switched over, when warm, to kerosene. In the Yamaha engine the changeover is automatic, continuous and gradual as the revs are increased; at idle, pure gasoline/oil is used and at full throttle pure kerosene/oil. Thus, to reap the economy of kerosene the motor must be run at around three-quarter throttle.

Another attractive idea from the economy and safety point of view is the diesel outboard. It is an idea that is feasible, and has been done albeit with severe penalties, such as noise, vibration and weight. One of the few diesels on the market is the Carniti 16 hp. This Italian motor weighs 260 pounds (120 kg) — about as much as a 80-hp conventional outboard—and naturally costs more than a conventional outboard of the same power. Although the much greater noise is a snag, the diesel is more reliable mainly because of the absence of electric ignition. Fuel consumption of the Carniti at full throttle is less than half that of a conventional outboard at full throttle, while at cruising speed this would reduce to one-third or one-quarter; diesel fuel is generally cheap, and considerably safer.

A propeller is not the only way of producing thrust, and there are one or two jet outboards. The Warrenjet (3-hp and 5-hp models), which is otherwise conventional, has a jet arrangement at the bottom of the leg: water is sucked up through a bell mouth and ejected backwards by an impeller inside the housing. The advantages are that with no external rotating parts it is a very safe motor when there are people in the water; there is no projection below the bottom of the boat when beaching it; there are no gears and consequently no gear oil to change. When pushing very slow, heavy boats there is no penalty in terms of thrust, but the nature of the drive of the Warrenjet precludes comparable efficiency in small, light and faster craft.

An altogether different sort of outboard is the electric outboard. Mercury, Johnson, Evinrude, Byrd Industries, The Eska Co., Jetco, Minn Kota, and Motor. Guide, among others, now offer at least one model. A small electric motor drives a propeller, the current coming from a car-type battery. The larger the battery the greater the range, but the power output available, because of the limited amount of energy capable of being stored in a battery, only provides around a tenth of the power of the smallest petrol outboard—roughly equivalent to that produced by a rower. Consequently one cannot regard electric outboards as an alternative to small gasoline ones. But used in calm, current-free water at slow speeds and on small boats, their advantages of absolute quietness, reliability, controllability and cleanliness make them useful for easily driven craft like canoes or rowboats, for fishing, or on very small cruisers. The fact that still water offers such a minute amount of resistance to motion at speeds of 2 to 3 knots (3.5 to 5.5 km/hr) allows these motors to be successful. One cannot expect electric outboards to give propulsion against strong winds or currents.

Future possibilities

What lies on the horizon in outboard motor development, especially those changes directly beneficial to the boat owner? The current concern over oil reserves and the environment may have considerable influence on future motor design. Just as manufacturers have successfully tackled the old bugbears of noise and unreliability, so they may turn their considerable talents to the question of fuel consumption and the related problem of exhaust emission. A large improvement can be achieved simply by changing to the four-stroke cycle, but if the weight and cost factors are intolerable, there are, currently under development for car engines, innovations to improve engine efficiency which could also be applied to two-stroke engines.

Great economy can be gained if an engine can be made to run on a 15:1 or 20:1 fuel/air mixture rather than the 8:1 or 12:1 common to outboards. A means of firing such weak mixtures is the problem, and maybe the stratified charge engine will come into production. (The mixture within the cylinder is arranged to be in alternate rich and weak layers, the area around the sparkplug being rich.) Plasma jet plugs in lieu of sparkplugs is another possibility; these would shoot a tongue of flame through a weak mixture. Gas injection is yet another possible, but expensive, development for outboard motors. There is a good chance of one or another radical innovation coming into production to reduce the fuel consumption, because there is still considerable scope for improvement.

To avoid having to mix the lubricating oil with the fuel, and also to satisfy environmental concern, it is possible to design a two-stroke with a lubrication system which is virtually separate from the combustion system, as in a four-stroke engine. A separate lube oil tank and pressure feed system is used on some Japanese motorcycles, and a new British Norton Villiers motorcycle now has a simple two-stroke engine which employs a stepped, double piston for induction, leaving the crankcase free for pressure lubrication. The engine thus runs on neat gasoline, and the oil is recirculated rather than deliberately burned.

Although the internal combustion engine for outboards is going to be with us for a long time, perhaps its fuel will change to bottled gas or hydrogen. Certainly the grading and leading of petroleum fuels is changing, and taxation patterns, which affect cost, are also altering in many countries.

Of more immediate concern, let us hope that outboards will become easier to maintain; in particular that the water pump is moved to an accessible position, bolted on to the power head for instance, and that the magneto is moved out from under the flywheel. One also hopes that outboards suited to pushing heavy boats along at displacement speeds will be developed. There has been a need for such a design for a long time, to serve as sailing yacht auxiliaries and for inland cruisers. The requisite features are a longer leg, a larger slow-revving propeller, and an electricity generator of bigger output. Some isolated motors do have some, but not all, of these qualities. Significantly, Chrysler has recently produced special sailboat motors with a large reduction ratio in the hub, able to swing a large propeller. And finally, it is time that outboard motors had a designed-in secure locking system, rather than leaving the owner to cope to the satisfaction of his insurance company.

How to Choose an Outboard

One has first to choose a suitable power, bearing in mind such things as the boat, its use and the cruising area, and then pick a particular make. The latter choice is more difficult; naturally one wants a reputable make with good spares and service back-up. Probably you could find owners (or previous owners) of any make who swear *by* their engine or *at* it, but on the other hand, it is true to say that the big makes are likely to be able to give good after-sales service because of their extensive network of dealers holding parts and employing factory trained mechanics. However, it is a fact of life that the bigger the firm, the more impersonal the service becomes.

To have to send the motor back and follow up by phone or letter is far less satisfactory than having a dealer down the road with whom you can establish a rapport and who you know holds a good stock of spares. New makes or ones that have just started to be imported are naturally suspect. Will it be a reliable motor? Are all spare parts available quickly? Will the importation of engines and spares suddenly cease? These are questions which the concessionaires are usually very much aware of, and they set up their service and spares system before selling the first motor. The question of service and parts is rather similar to the situation with cars: to some extent you have to cross your fingers and hope. But the least one can do is to find out where spares are obtainable (ask for particular items like a water pump impeller or an ignition coil) and where the outboard itself can be serviced or repaired.

Now suppose you have in front of you the glossy brochures of various makes: inside, there is usually a table giving technical details. How can one use these figures in order to compare makes? Such things as weight are straightforward, but cylinder capacity, for instance, is one technical item that often does not allow comparison. In comparing the cylinder capacities of different makes of the same horsepower, peculiar anomalies will often be found. In the smaller sizes there is one motor that has twice the capacity of another of the same nominal power, and among the various 50- to 55-hp makes, capacity ranges from 600 cc to 824 cc. Another peculiarity that can be found is that within one make the 40-hp engine has a greater capacity than the 50-hp unit. Also within one make, identical cylinder bore and stroke measurements appear on motors of three different horsepower ratings. In all these (real) instances, the motors are of conventional two-stroke design.

Such anomalies are not the result of vastly different recommended rpm ranges, as one might expect, so either the horsepower rating quoted is nominal or pessimistic (bearing in mind earlier remarks), or the tuning and carburetion differ. Test results suggest that the big capacity, less highly tuned motor does not necessarily give better performance in terms of fuel economy at part throttle as one might expect. In other words, the higher rated or comparatively low capacity motor gives better cruising

The boat is well-balanced and adequately powered, but the single V-6 should be accompanied by a small "get home" kicker for safety in off-shore work.

Top speed performance of equally rated outboards is the same, but tests show that engines with a larger capacity handle loads with better acceleration.

consumption. On the other hand, tests on planing boats tend to show that the bigger capacity motor gives less drop-off of speed as the load on the boat increases (passengers or skiers), and there seems to be a greater margin of power available at the planing speed hump although the top-speed performance is much the same.

Newly introduced models often appear to be out of step with their neighbors in the same maker's range, and tests do generally show that such engines perform better than their elders.

Other technical details like gear ratio, propeller size, cooling and ignition systems are usually given, and the following summary of worthwhile features is a guide for students of the glossy brochures.

Single or multiple cylinders: the more cylinders an engine has the smoother it will run; if the ignition is separate for each cylinder it will continue running if one cylinder stops firing.

Fuel/oil ratio specified: the less oil in the mixture the cleaner the engine will run. This means fewer sparkplug changes, a cleaner exhaust, and less chance of plug fouling on continuous slow running. Mixture commonly varies between 10:1 and 50:1.

In boats steered from an aft cockpit, the view forward is sometimes restricted. A careful watch must be kept for floating debris.

Water or oil cooling: water cooling usually makes for a quieter engine, but there is a water pump impeller to go wrong and blockage of the intake or water passages is possible. If this happens without your knowledge the engine may overheat and seize up. A thermostat keeps the temperature up, prolongs engine life, and promotes combustion efficiency.

Large gear ratio: the slower the designed maximum speed of the boat the greater the desirability of a large propeller, which implies a large reduction ratio; 2.5:1 is good, 1.5:1 poor. The difference in performance for displacement boats is very noticeable, while a good reduction ratio is still advantageous even at 20 knots. At speeds over 30 knots the reverse becomes true because of the drag of the bigger hub. For pulling skiers out of the water a good reduction is very desirable. (Gear ratios are often expressed as the ratio of the number of teeth on the gears, e.g. 13:26 = 2:1 or 12:30 = 2.5:1.

CD ignition: capacitor-discharge ignition is definitely superior in terms of good starting and less plug trouble and maintenance, but if something does go wrong it is a job for the dealer. There is no chance of putting matters right at sea: on the other hand, there should be less chance that it will go wrong. Some CD systems retain the contact breaker which is the feature of conventional flywheel magneto ignition. Flywheel magnetos give a less powerful spark, so there is little margin for dirty points or plugs or aged or partially shorted coils. The ignition system is probably the cause of most outboard breakdowns.

Underwater exhaust, sealed hoods, rubber mounts, intake silencer, water cooling: all play their part in the making of a quiet motor.

Modern designs: test results indicate that *new* models (as opposed to yearly re-vamped engines) give better fuel consumption for their horsepower than older designs.

Surface-gap plugs: compared to the conventional side-electrode plug these are less sensitive to fouling—as when slow running—but are sometimes less readily available and are more expensive.

Slim underwater designs: drag of the lower unit is very important on planing boats. It's difficult to tell how "draggy" a particular motor is, but one can compare it with a big make which claims computer-designed low-drag legs.

Automatic rewind starter: much less frustrating than the old notched pulley and starting cord system, but if the cord or spring breaks more difficult to mend.

Splined prop shaft: no shear pin to replace when the propeller hits an obstruction.

Number of carburetors: for performance and efficiency, more than one carburetor on multi-cylinder engines is advantageous.

This small 35-hp outboard is having no trouble towing an adult skier. In such a situation, the prop should be pitched for power in the lower rpm range, to facilitate getting over the hump.

ne per cylinder is the ideal, but multi-carburetors need expert attention when tuning because it is essential that they be correctly balanced so that each delivers the same fuel/air charge. *Fixed jets:* no mixture controls on the front of the motor to have to fiddle with (or to accidentally upset).

Weight: whether you will want a really lightweight motor depends on how much man-handling is envisaged, and also the size and speed of your boat. The faster and the smaller the boat the greater the importance of a light motor.

Integral transom lock: not often fitted, but becoming an essential feature. Insurance companies often will not insure (or pay up) unless the motor is properly locked to the boat.

Electric generator or electric starting: make sure the option exists on the chosen make if you want it now or possibly in the future. Also make sure that charging starts at low revs if the motor is usually to be run slowly.

In addition, decide whether you want a long or short shaft (or ultra-long), reverse gears or 360° pivot or a clutch, and whether you want to get away from the two-stroke cycle and go for a four-stroke.

One of the simplest rigs going—a moderate-sized outboard engine on an open, center-console deep-V planing hull.

The Right Outboard
for Your Boat

The fast, open runabout—or speedboat, ski-boat, sports boat—is ideally powered by an outboard motor. Compared to an inboard or even an outdrive (inboard–outboard) they are very light, do not take up space inside the boat, and constitute the simplest and least expensive power plant. Light weight is absolutely vital to the performance of any planing boat, especially for small speedboats 10 to 18 feet long. The top speed of such boats is mainly dictated by the power:weight ratio. Other factors such as hull form pale into relative insignificance alongside this one unalterable phenomenon. The power to weight ratio is often expressed as so many horsepower per ton weight, but because speedboats usually weigh less than one ton it is more convenient to talk of horsepower per 100 pounds (or hp per 100 kg). The weight of importance is the *actual* weight of the boat skimming along at X knots, including its motor, crew, fuel and gear. The graph was drawn up using the top-speed results of forty or fifty open speedboats ranging from 10 to 18 feet in length and having various hull forms. Each of these had only one person on board, and did not have any inherent faults such as the wrong propeller or a fouled bottom or an incorrect motor tilt angle.

One can use this graph to illustrate how important weight is for small speedboats. Many people are tempted to fit a diesel outdrive to overcome the high fuel consumption and cost of outboards; for a 16-foot boat with a 35-hp outboard, the build-up of weight would be roughly as follows:

boat including seats, steering gear, etc.	600 lb.	275 kg
gear including anchor, etc.	60	27
outboard	110	50
tank and some fuel	35	16
one person	150	68
	955 lb.	436 kg

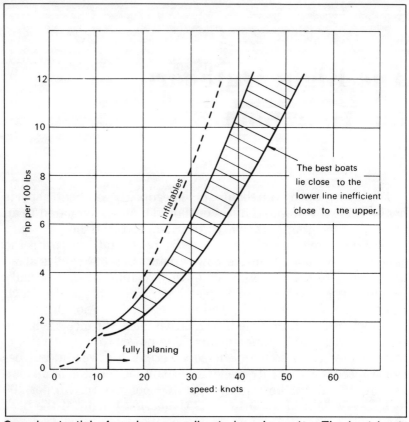

Speed potential of modern speedboats in calm water. The best boats lie close to the lower line, the inefficient close to the upper. Weight is the combined load of boat, motor, crew, tank and gear; hp is the nominal horsepower of the motor.

This gives 3.7 hp per 100 pounds (8.2 hp/100 kg) and consequently about 26 knots (48 km/hr) top speed and a sparkling performance, easy planing over the hump, and a margin for towing one or two skiers or for extra passengers.

Now consider a diesel outdrive installation of approximately equivalent power. A high-revving and relatively lightweight diesel which could be used is the BLMC 1.5 liter giving 38 hp at 3500 rpm. For a diesel it is lightweight, but compared to an outboard the figures speak for themselves:

boat (as above)	600 lb.	275 kg
gear (as above)	60	27
engine	453	207
outdrive	90	41

battery	50	23
engine bearers	40	18
tank and fuel	35	16
exhaust system	20	9
one person	150	68
	1498 lb.	684 kg

The overall increase is in the order of 50 percent, equivalent to permanently carrying about four extra passengers in the stern. The top speed shown by the graph is now only about 20 knots (37 km/hr), i.e. 2.5 hp per 100 pounds or 5.5 hp per 100 kg, but just as important, the extra weight in the stern would make rising over the hump and on to the plane very difficult. There would be little margin for passengers or a fouled bottom, and towing skiers would be out of the question. The diesel would inevitably be noisy and take up a large slice of the cockpit. A bigger diesel with outdrive would increase the power:weight ratio but at the expense of an even greater trim by the stern, and would add just too much weight for the hull. An inboard drive arrangement through a shaft would make for better weight distribution, but the all-up weight of the boat may by this time be just too heavy for the area of planing surface: there is a limit to the weight-lifting capability of a fixed planing area. Larger boats can be successfully diesel driven because the weight of the engine in relation to the all-up weight becomes less significant: the crossover point occurs at a boat length of somewhere around 20.

A compromise between the economical but heavy diesel and the thirsty but light outboard lies in the gasoline outdrive. For our 16-foot boat one could consider an 1100 cc Ford engine working through an outdrive; indeed the combination of gasoline inboard with outdrive is frequently used in speedboats. The weight build-up would be roughly as follows:

boat	600 lb.	275 kg
gear	60	27
engine	300	137
outdrive	90	41
battery	25	11
engine bearers	30	14
tank and fuel	35	16
exhaust system	20	9
one person	150	68
	1310 lb.	598 kg

This particular engine develops about 42 hp at 4500 rpm, which

would give 3.2 hp per 100 pounds (7 hp/100 kg) and a performance not far off that of the 35-hp outboard. The advantages of an outdrive over an outboard are potentially greater reliability, no possibility of theft of the motor and less fuel consumption, but of course the initial and installation costs are higher. Fuel has to be burned to carry the extra weight around, so the economy advantage of the four-stroke cycle is partially lost, as the following test figures show.

Two identical 18-foot fiberglass boats (actually with a small cabin) were tested together; one had a 135-hp outboard and one a 140-hp outdrive, both of the same make. The top speeds achieved were 36.7 knots (68 km/hr) for the outboard and 32.9 knots (61 km/hr.) for the outdrive, after each had run 60 hours from new. The corresponding all-up weights were 1900 pounds (870 kg) and 2400 pounds (1100 kg). To overcome the planing hump, more revs were required in the case of the outdrive. The two boats were always run in company. A third of the time was spent at a cruising speed of about 20 knots (37 km/hr), about half the time at slow speeds, and the rest at high revs, the outdrive running slightly less time at full throttle: a rather typical usage pattern. The resulting fuel consumption after 100 hours total running time was 270 gallons (1,020 L) for the outboard and 245 gallons (930 L) for the outdrive. In normal pleasure boat usage 100 hours represents one or two seasons, while it can be seen that the saving in fuel cost with the outdrive is not all that much, and it would take many seasons of use to amortize its higher initial cost.

In conclusion one can say that the outboard motor's extreme lightness makes it an almost unbeatable power plant for small speedboats.

Suitable power

The size of outboard you buy for your speedboat must of course depend on your pocket, but it is no use buying one that is too small and will not make the boat plane. Obviously, for each size of boat there is a certain minimum power, and a clue to this minimum can be gleaned from the speed graph. As a general guide, 2.5 hp per 100 pounds (5.5 hp/100 kg) is the lower limit for successful planing. Having mentioned the "hump" several

To facilitate spotting fish, this fishing boat has a tuna tower with its own helm station, including throttle, wheel, and essential instruments.

times already, its significance is probably apparent. It is a phenomenon which stems from the wave-making of a hull being pushed through the water: the hump is the critical speed at which the waves created behind the boat are at their largest and the drag on the boat reaches a peak (5). If the engine has

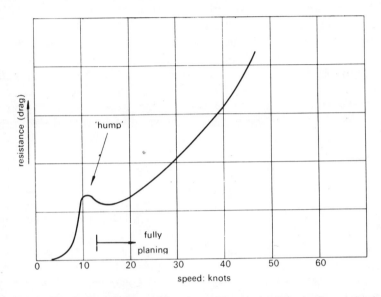

Typical speedboat drag in calm water. The motor has to force the boat over the hump to start it planing.

enough power in hand it can push the boat a little faster, and suddenly the waves are left behind and the boat starts skimming over the water on its flat bottom. For speedboats the hump occurs at around 10 knots (18 km/hr). An outboard or any engine driving a fixed propeller suffers a disadvantage at the hump because the revs are held down by the low speed of the boat. Consequently the full power of the engine is not available. Once over the hump, the boat accelerates away and the revs rise.

The onset of planing is made more difficult by extra passengers or weight, a fouled bottom or a strong headwind, by a too-large propeller or simply a badly tuned engine. From tests on 14- to 16-foot boats, it appears that for each passenger added, roughly, $1\frac{1}{2}$ knots (3 km/hr) are lost, but things may become more critical at the hump if a minimum-sized motor is used. Also, for reasonable fuel consumption it is often better to have

Once over the hump and on a plane, a boat's wetted surface is substantially reduced. The prop is then free to wind up, and the engine to reach maximum rpm.

a bigger motor and cruise at somewhat less than full throttle (still planing), rather than a smaller motor running at full throttle. A deep-V hull takes much more power to coax on to the plane than a flat-bottomed one, so a good margin is necessary with such boats.

The previously mentioned figure of 2.5 hp per 100 pounds (5.5 hp/100 kg) does give a little margin, but not very much. This figure should be applied to the weight of the whole outfit, i.e. boat plus gear plus outboard plus one or two people. Doubling up the power to 5 hp per 100 pounds 11 hp/kg) gives a very good margin, and a lively boat with good acceleration. To give a scale to these figures, the maximum that is normally used on "family" boats is 7.5 hp per 100 pounds (16.5 hp/100 kg), but before turning to the question of maximum *safe* power the following relationship between speedboat length and outboard horsepower gives a very rough idea of the value of 2.5 hp per 100 pounds:

Length in ft. (m)	Motor hp
10 (3)	10
12 (3.7)	15
14 (4.3)	20
16 (4.9)	30
18 (5.5)	40

Because so many variables are involved, such as the efficiency of the chosen outboard and the hull form, it is advisable to work out a horsepower from the figure of 2.5 hp per 100 pounds using the afloat weight of the particular boat, as well as the maximum safe horsepower, in order to give a range of possible powers for your particular boat.

Turning now to the *maximum* power one can safely put in a speedboat, the best recommendations to follow are those put forward by the Federal Boat Safety Act. The greater the power installed the greater the chance of the craft coming to grief through the sheer forces created by that power. The thrust from the propeller is well below the hull, which means that there is a chance of it somersaulting over backwards if the throttle is suddenly opened with the boat stationary. Chine tripping becomes more of a possibility at higher speeds: this is the digging-in of the chine in a tight turn, causing the boat to capsize. Shallow-V or flat-bottomed boats are more prone to do this than those with deep-V hulls. There is the third possibility, with a big heavy motor weighing the stern down together with low freeboard across the transom, of the boat being swamped by its own stern wave when the throttle is closed suddenly. Consequently the regulations take into account the transom height and whether the bottom is flat or not, and also whether remote controls are fitted. Outboards of over about 30 hp become rather cumbersome to handle by tiller alone, and wheel steering with a separate throttle puts the helmsman in better control of the boat, and his weight where it will help to counterbalance the engine weight.

A factor is calculated from the overall length of the boat in feet multiplied by the width of the transom in feet (excluding any rubbing strips or fins). The maximum horsepower permitted is then:

Factor	0–35	36–39	40–42	43–45	46–52
hp	3	5	$7\frac{1}{2}$	10	15

If the measurements are in meters, after multiplying the length and width together multiply by 10. For flat-bottomed, hard-chine boats reduce the hp capacity by one increment (e.g. from $7\frac{1}{2}$ to 5 hp).

If the factor turns out to be more than 52 and the boat has remote steering and a 20-inch (500 mm) transom height, the hp capacity is (2 × Factor) − 90; without remote steering or if transom height is under 20 inches the hp capacity is (0.8 × Factor) − 25; if the boat is also flat-bottomed, (0.5 × Factor)

— 15. The safe hp capacity so calculated can be raised to the nearest multiple of 5. For example, a boat 16 feet (5 m) long × 5 feet (1.5 m) in width at the transom with a 15-inch (380 mm) transom height (i.e. taking a short-shaft motor) has a maximum capacity of $(0.8 \times 16 \times 5) - 25 = 39$ hp, i.e. 40 hp. A motor well with watertight inner bulkhead giving good freeboard counts as a 20-inch transom, so in this case the maximum capacity works out at $(2 \times 16 \times 5) - 90 = 70$ hp.

The graph shows the approximate speed obtained from various sizes of outboards on a Morebas 17-foot (5.2 m) runabout. One can see that with the smaller sizes of outboards passenger load becomes critical, and it pays to choose an outboard well above the minimum necessary for planing with a light load. As a final thought on the subject, another rough guide to the *minimum* satisfactory power is to choose an outboard which gives a speed of at least 20 knots.

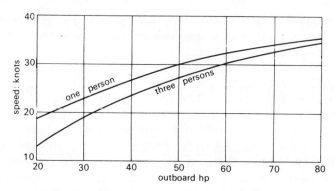

Effect of load on a 17-foot (5.2 m) speedboat.

For the maximum power a safe guide is the U.S. regulation outlined above, but in capable hands a suitable boat can take a greater power—but then the responsibility is yours, and that is exactly how a court of law might look upon the matter if damage or injury should occur.

Mounting

Most outboard manufacturers conform to two standard transom heights: 15 inches (380 mm) for short-shaft and 20 inches (500 mm) for long-shaft motors, although some are slightly different. The meaning of transom height is shown in the diagram. All boats should have corresponding transom heights, because the

The outboard is positioned so the cavitation plate is level with the bottom of the transom, avoiding both drag from the leg and, at speed, ventilation.

whole purpose of this standard height business is to ensure that the propeller of any outboard comes at the correct height relative to the bottom of the hull. This position is critical: If the propeller is too high the water flow into it will be blanked off, while if it is too low there will be more leg to drag through the water. Better to be on the low side than the high. Generally the cavitation plate should be on a level with the bottom of the transom. If there is a small keel or skeg stopping within a few inches of the transom the outboard is better lowered so that the cavitation plate is level with the underside of it. But the more leg exposed the greater the parasitic drag, and this becomes more and more important the faster the boat. For speeds over 30 knots (55 km/hr) it is worthwhile experimenting, packing the motor up higher by inserting slips of wood on top of the transom. When the propeller is too high ventilation (engine racing with loss of thrust) will take place at high speeds.

The tables give the dimensions of the motor well necessary to allow full tilt and turn, with remote control cables attached, of current model outboards. A 20-inch (500 mm) transom height should be achieved on any boat using 30 hp or over unless there is a motor well.

Holes in the well for cables should be as small and as high

up as possible, and the inner bulkhead should slope aft to deflect wave slap aft, rather than forward. As a precaution, where there is a seat across the front of the well another 3 inches (75 mm) should be added to dimension E to avoid a passenger's arm being caught if the outboard tilts up suddenly.

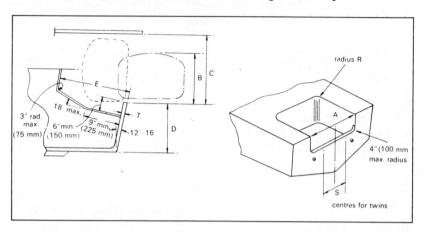

Motor well dimensions:

Motor hp	T in. (mm) min.	T in. (mm) max.	B in. (mm)	C in. (mm)	E in. (mm)
under 5½	1¼ (32)	1¾ (44)	14 (350)	18 (460)	21½ (545)
5½–12	1⅜ (35)	1¾ (44)	17 (400)	22½ (570)	21½ (545)
12–61	1⅜ (35)	2 (50)	21 (530)	29 (740)	21½ (545)
61–91	1⅝ (41)	2¼ (57)	28 (710)	32½ (830)	24 (610)
91+	1⅝ (41)	2¼ (57)	28 (710)	32½ (830)	30 (760)

D can be either 14½–15 inches (370–380 nm) short-shaft, or 19½–20 inches (495–510 mm) long-shaft, but if the boat is intended for motors of 61 hp or over the transom height D should be the nominal 20 inches. For motors of 30 to 60 hp the transom height should also be 20 inches, unless there is a self-bailing well. Remote steering should be used for motors of over 30 hp.

Motor hp	A in. (mm) single	A in. (mm) twin	S in. (mm)	R in. (mm)
under 61	33 (840)	54 (1375)	22 (560)	15 (380)
61 + hp	33 (840)	60 (1510)	26 (660)	20 (550)

The width A for twin motors assumes that the motors are spaced according to S. In the case of a deep-V hull designed for twin or a single motor, a straight top to the transom can often be arranged by adopting a spacing S for twins that suits short-shaft twins or a long-shaft single. Otherwise steps in the top of the transom have to be cut.

Required size of mounting pads on transom:

	On after face of transom		On forward face of transom	
	width	depth	width	depth
Motor hp	in. (mm)	in. (mm)	in. (mm)	in. (mm)
under 5½	9½ (240)	7¼ (185)	7½ (190)	3 (76)
5½–12	13 (330)	7¼ (185)	8½ (215)	4¾ (120)
12–50	13 (330)	10½ (265)	10¾ (275)	4¾ (120)
50+	15¾ (400)	14 (350)	15¾ (400)	4⅛ (105)

Where an outboard is supplied with bolt holes in the mounting bracket (usually over 40 hp), it should be bolted in place in addition to the clamp screws. Bolting is also a good precaution for small motors.

The thrust generated by the propeller is quite considerable in the case of larger outboards, as will be appreciated after reading the static thrust test figures below in the section on skiing.

Being situated so low, the propeller thrust puts a large twisting force on the top of the transom via the clamp. This must be resisted by a correspondingly strong and well-braced transom, and a guide is provided by Det Norske Veritas rules for fiberglass boats with a plywood sandwich transom:

Up to 40 hp	¾–1 in. (20–25 mm) core thickness
40–80 hp	1–1¼ in. (25–30 mm) core thickness
80–130 hp	1¼–1⅜ in. (30–35 mm) core thickness

The fiberglass laminate on each side of the plywood should be as thick as the hull sides.

Small motors of up to say 6 hp need nothing more special in the way of transom stiffening than is normally fitted to strengthen the boat, apart from a pad to take the screw clamps. The thrust of a 20-hp motor is at the most about 300 pounds (135 kg)—the weight of two men—which is not a very great force, but does need consideration when one is completing a bare fiberglass hull. The twist on the transom can be taken out by a vertical plank fastened from top to bottom of the transom on the centerline. The outboard also pushes forwards via its clamp screws, consequently tending to bend the gunwale across the top of the transom: this item also needs to be able to withstand the 300-pound forward push. If the two sides are taken down to the boat's bottom, a well will strengthen the transom enormously in this respect. An aft deck or large quarter knees on each side of the transom also help.

To take the sharp edges or serrations of the bracket and the indentation of the clamp screws, plywood pads should be fitted on each side of the transom (see chart for sizes). It is important that the outer surfaces are soft to some degree, to reduce the chance of the screws working loose and the outboard consequently falling off the boat.

When the wheel is put over and the throttle simultaneously opened, there is a large athwartships twisting moment applied to the clamp screws. If one clamp screw has shaken loose through vibration the whole motor will swivel sideways around the tight one, which means that it may drop overboard. Tying the toggles of the two clamp screws together is a solution only for small motors, and anything over about 15 hp should be through-bolted to the transom. The larger outboards have holes for this purpose in their mounting brackets. The bolts may be stainless steel or galvanized mild steel. A locknut on each is a good precaution against loosening by vibration, and bedding compound will seal the holes against water leakage.

Trimming for Performance

A speedboat is the waterborne equivalent of a sports car, and it needs to be as carefully tuned, and kept tuned, if the best per-

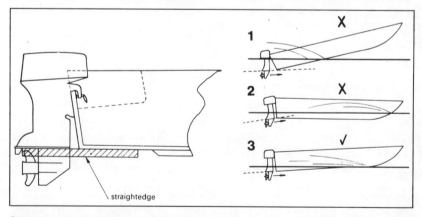

Correct motor height and tilt are important: check that cavitation plate is level and parallel with the bottom of the boat, using a straightedge. An incorrect motor tilt angle affects boat trim: *1* can cause porpoising and cavitation at the hump; *2* creates extra drag from added wetted surface.

formance is to be achieved. Tuning a speedboat does not mean simply fiddling with the carburetor of the motor: there are many ways in which performance can be improved.

As well as the height of the outboard in relation to the transom, the correct angle of tilt is an important point. There is normally an adjustment rack on the clamp bracket, so this is a simple matter, but it's frequently overlooked. The aim is to set the motor so that the cavitation plate is parallel to the bottom of the hull, looking at the boat sideways on. However it is worth a little experimentation on trials to determine the best rack position, because the trim (the fore-and-aft attitude in the water) is also affected. At planing speeds the angle of the bottom planing surface (in the fore-and-aft direction) to the horizontal should be from 4° for a flat-bottomed boat to 6° or so for a deep-V hull. This angle is fairly critical as regards the resistance of the hull. As speedboats normally have fixed seats, there is little that can be done by shifting crew weight around.

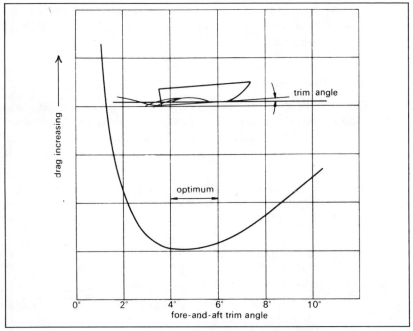

The effect of incorrect trim at high speed, especially a too-flat angle. Motor tilt affects boat trim.

Nor would one want to add ballast, so the remaining variable is the tilt of the outboard or possibly trim tabs. When experi-

menting with the outboard tilt position an accurate speedometer is vital to detect small changes in the top speed, and
with it the best tilt position is easily determined. The performance at the hump is very much affected by the motor tilt
position. If the outboard is in a rack position such that it is
tilted aft, the propeller will be pushing slightly downwards and
at the hump the bow will rise to a greater extent and the propeller may cavitate. As I said above, in general the best rack
position is such that the cavitation plate is parallel with the
bottom of the hull, and this can be checked with a straight
plank.

The rack adjustment can be used to reduce or stop porpoising—the regular rhythmic pitching of a planing boat which
is caused by running at too great a trim angle. Experimenting
with the rack position should show that tilting the outboard
forward (i.e. using a more forward rack position) and consequently causing the propeller to thrust slightly upwards, thus
lifting the stern, reduces porpoising. Bigger motors can be fitted
with a remotely controlled power-trim device so that the motor
can be trimmed in to make getting past the hump easier (or
when pulling skiers up) or to reduce slamming in rough water,
or trimmed out for more speed in calm water conditions.

Other prerequisites for the best performance are a clean
hook-free bottom, a smooth unchipped propeller, the correct
propeller, and of course an unladen boat. If the boat is normally
kept ashore then there is no problem in keeping the bottom
smooth, but otherwise antifouling, even in fresh water, pays off.
The outboard should be left tilted up out of the water for the
same reason, apart from eliminating the possibility of water getting into the gear casing, and reducing corrosion. In coastal
waters fouling can reduce the top speed quite markedly within
a season, while in warmer waters the rate of fouling can be so
rapid that without antifouling, boats have failed to get up on
the plane after a few weeks' growth.

Boats left on ill-designed trailers or on small, badly positioned chocks can have their bottoms permanently hooked or
kinked, and this has been known to seriously affect performance. The weight of the boat should be taken at the keel and
chines and well distributed.

Correct propeller size

I have left till last what is perhaps the most important tuning
factor—the correct propeller—simply the one that will allow

the engine to rev up to its full rated rpm at full throttle. It is as simple as that, but the only way to check what is happening is to fit a tachometer (rev counter). These are readily available and easy to fit, and not too expensive. Most of the big outboard makes have them on their accessory lists. A tachometer is really an essential item on a fast boat; it shows immediately whether the right propeller is fitted, and enables one to avoid overloading or overspeeding the motor. Overspeeding causes excessive wear, while overloading (due to a too-large propeller preventing the motor reaching its rated rpm) causes carbon build-up, pre-ignition, overheating with scored cylinder walls, and even burned-out pistons.

The correct full-throttle operating range of revs is usually stated by the manufacturer (e.g. 4000 to 5000 rpm) and the full horsepower is usually attained at mid-range (in this case 4500

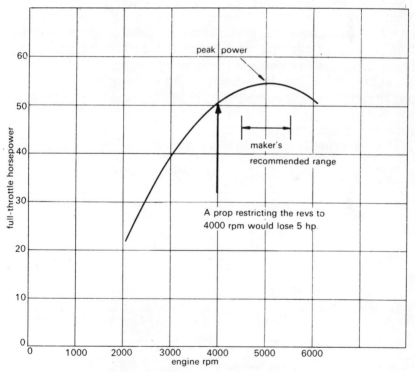

Typical power curve of an outboard.

Note that on this engine, the exhaust exits from a nozzle just below the cavitation plate. This drastically reduces ventilation when powering in reverse.

rpm). It is important to run within this range at full throttle to achieve the best power output from the engine. Power drops off on either side of the optimum rpm.

Unfortunately, the loading of the boat will affect the full-throttle rpm achieved, so one must check the rpm with the tachometer and fit a propeller suited to the most common load, and then at lighter or heavier loads make sure that the engine does not race or labor too much. Both conditions are very detrimental to engine life.

Apart from loading, air temperature and pressure affect the power and rpm. At higher temperatures and lower pressures the air becomes less dense, and the actual weight of air sucked into the cylinders at each revolution gets less. Consequently the amount of fuel that can be burned, and the power produced, falls off. For a fall in barometer pressure of 1 in of mercury (34 mB) the power falls by 4 percent while a rise of 10°F (5.5°C) causes a loss of 2 percent. Similarly, if a motor is run on a lake well above sea level, a drop of 4 percent for every 1000 feet (300 m) of altitude can be expected. In fact the losses are, if anything, greater because these figures assume that the revs are kept constant, i.e. that the propeller is changed for a smaller one that restores the correct revs. Humidity also plays a part, so the best performance will be achieved on a cold, humid day with high barometric pressure.

The following test results show the effect of propeller choice

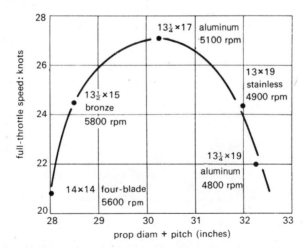

Speed is lost with incorrectly sized propellers. Correct revs for this 60-hp Johnson outboard are 5000 rpm full throttle.

on performance. The boat was a standard Dell Quay Dory running in calm water with four people on board, powered by a 60-hp Johnson. All-up weight was 2070 pounds (940 kg). Five different propellers were fitted and the top speeds timed over a measured course. On this graph (11), alongside each spot (representing one propeller) is the full-throttle rpm achieved, which gradually rises as the propeller size reduces. (A smaller propeller puts less load on the engine and hence it revs higher.) For propeller size a rough guide is to use a figure of propeller diameter plus propeller pitch in inches (e.g. 14 × 14 = size 28). The Johnson 60 develops its full power at 5000 rpm, and it is around this rpm that the maximum boat speed was achieved. The optimum propeller which held the engine to this rpm was in fact an ordinary aluminum three-blader. The other propellers were either too small or too big, and lost up to 6 knots (11 km/hr) of speed.

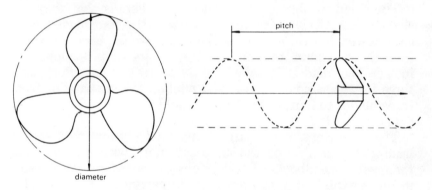

Diameter and pitch of a propeller. The pitch is the distance it would screw itself through the water in one complete revolution assuming there was no slip (due to being a liquid medium). Diameter and pitch figures are often stamped on the boss, otherwise there is a manufacturer's code number.

The principal features of a propeller that load an engine are the diameter and pitch; other things such as the number of blades or the material have much less influence. The most important thing in propeller selection is to ensure that the engine will reach its rated rpm at full throttle with the chosen propeller. In these tests the other more expensive bronze and four-bladed propellers gave a poorer performance than the relatively cheap aluminum one, simply because they happened to be the wrong size. A bronze or stainless steel or Teflon coated propeller of the same size and shape as the optimum propeller should give a slightly better speed. Stronger materials allow thinner blade sections and thus greater efficiency, but it is clear that such extra efficiency is of no use if the propeller is the wrong size.

A four-bladed propeller is only useful where there is insufficient total blade area on a three-blader to avoid cavitation at full throttle. Any propeller can only give a certain amount of thrust: if turned faster and faster and held back in the water by a "draggy" boat, there comes a time when there is a sudden thrust breakdown and the engine races. This is the result of cavitation. A propeller works by lowering the water pressure on the front faces of the blades and increasing it on the back faces. In fact most of the work is done by the suction on the forward faces. Cavitation starts when this approaches zero (a pure vacuum) and cavities are formed in the water flowing over the front faces of the blades.

The disadvantage of four-bladed propellers is that they are slightly less efficient. In the above test the four-bladed prop gave fewer full-throttle revs than one would have expected from the maximum revs achieved by the other propellers, and in fact four blades do take slightly more turning effort than three for the same diameters and pitches. When changing from three blades to four, about 1 inch should be taken off the size of diameter + pitch (expressed in inches).

The conditions of high thrust at relatively low boat speeds leading to possible cavitation occur more with slower boats than with speedboats. There might be occasions—when surmounting the hump, towing skiers or carrying a heavy load—when cavitation occurs, but if a wider blade, three-bladed or a four-bladed propeller is fitted the top speed will suffer. Two blades offer better efficiency for really fast boats of over about 40 knots, but as for the vast majority of speedboats they cannot give enough area to prevent cavitation, and in general three blades are best.

Bronze and stainless-steel propellers also offer better resistance to the effects of cavitation and accidental damage, and they are more readily repaired than those of die-cast aluminum. The sort of cavitation mentioned results in a dramatic loss of thrust and violent engine racing, but in fact at high throttle openings some unnoticeable degree of cavitation is quite likely, and the

The first rule of skiing is that at least two people should be in the tow boat: the passenger is there to keep an alert watch on the skiers.

effects over a season or two can be seen as pitting on the forward faces of the blades. Harder materials generally resist this attack better than softer ones. Similar pitting can also occur through electrolytic corrosion if the leg is left down when the boat is not in use, though on both surfaces.

Like two-bladed propellers, cupped-edge propellers can give one or two extra knots to very fast speedboats. The cupped edge puts additional load on the engine, so the propeller size has to be reduced by about 1 inch, preferably on the pitch.

Most manufacturers offer a range of propeller sizes and types: the larger the outboard the larger the range. Their authorized dealers should be able to make a good stab at the optimum propeller, but inevitably there will be room for experimentation and the ultimate choice of a slightly better propeller. In order to satisfy the criterion that the engine reaches its rated rpm at full throttle, the faster the potential top speed of the boat powered by that engine the larger the propeller size has to be. In fact the diameter may reduce slightly, but the pitch will increase rapidly. For each boat and motor combination and thus for each achieved top speed there is a definite optimum propeller size, but as the actual speed you will get is questionable until the first trials, manufacturers usually list their propellers in relation to different types of boat rather than speeds. For example a typical list for a 50-hp motor might be:

Diameter in. (mm)	Pitch in. (mm)	No. of blades	Suitable for	Indicating a max. speed of about
14 (355)	9 (230)	4	heavy cruisers	7 knots (13 km/h)
14 (355)	9 (230)	3		
14 (355)	11 (280)	3	20–24 ft. (6–7 m) boats	12–15 knots (22–28 km/hr)
14 (355)	13 (330)	3	14–16 ft. (4.5–5 m) boats	20–25 knots (37–46 km/hr)
13½ (340)	15 (380)	3		
13¼ (335)	17 (430)	3	high speed	30–35 knots (55–65 km/hr)
13 (330)	19 (480)	3		
12¾ (325)	21 (530)	3	racing	40 knots (72 km/hr)
12½ (320)	23 (580)	2		

At trolling speeds, a large engine will run inefficiently and it may succumb to carbon build-up and over-heating; its best to use a trolling motor.

Authorized dealers *should* have such a list for each size of motor, making it a simple matter to pick a propeller which should be about right. Thereafter it is up to the owner to check the full-throttle rpm and if necessary choose a propeller either the next size up (i.e. of greater pitch) if the revs are too high, or the next size down if the revs are too low.

Steering effects

Cavitation is often induced in a tight turn: the boat's speed drops off and the propeller is suddenly more heavily loaded. But it can also be induced by turbulent water being shed into the propeller disc, from a keel or skeg ending for instance. If there is a keel it should end one or two feet forward of the transom, and if it cannot be cut farther back to overcome the cavitation problem then the answer may be to lower the outboard an inch or so.

Sometimes a speedboat tends to pull to one side, and this can be corrected by the trim tab that some makers fit to the underside of the cavitation plate. It is slackened off, turned slightly and tightened up again by trial and error. Otherwise one can swivel or slide the motor sideways across the transom so that the propeller is slightly off the centerline. If the boat steers to port move the motor to port, and vice versa. The steering wheel should be positioned to the side so that the helmsman's weight will help to counteract propeller torque reaction. With a right-handed propeller (prop turns clockwise when going ahead, viewed from astern) the wheel should be to starboard and vice versa.

The more powerful the motor the stronger the steering system must be, because very large forces are induced in the cables when maneuvering at high speed. Single push-pull cable steering (e.g. Morse Teleflex) should generally be fitted in preference to wire cable and pulleys: for one thing, there is always the danger that a wire running around a pulley may wear and eventually break. Large diameter pulleys (2 inch (50 mm) at least) help to prolong cable life and reduce friction. Double or triple purchase systems should be fitted for larger motors.

Outboard boat performances

The following graphs show the fuel consumption and speeds of four typical speedboats tested in calm water, with various hull shapes and increasing weight. Although the outboards may not be the very latest models, the trend of the curves is still valid. For instance mpg (km/L) fuel curves always show a dip at around the hump, where very uneconomical progress is made. The engine works hard but the boat digs her heels in just prior to planing. For 12- to 18-foot speedboats this dip in the consumption curve always occurs at between 6 and 11 knots (11 to 20 km/hr). Obviously this is a condition best avoided. On the other hand, there is an optimum cruising speed when the boat is planing properly but the motor is by no means at full throttle. Again this is a feature due to the boat rather than the outboard, and the economical speed lies between 16 and 22 knots

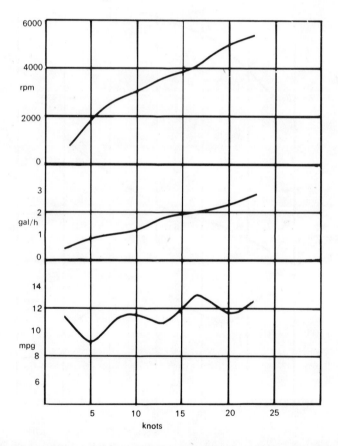

10-foot 9-inch (3.6 m) Bombard inflatable speedboat in calm water; trial weight 285 pounds (130 kg) plus two crew. Evinrude 25 hp at 5500 rpm; 360 cc (22 cu. in.), two cylinders, magneto ignition, 1.75:1 gear reduction.

(30 to 40 km/hr). Full throttle is always an expensive luxury, and a rule of thumb is that larger outboards consume 1.2 gallons (4.5 L) per hour for every 10 hp. In contrast, at the economical speed the consumption per hour is usually halved. The hump is evident in both the consumption-per-hour curves and the rpm curves. It usually takes quite high revs and a heavy hand on the throttle to push a boat over the hump, particularly deep-V hulls

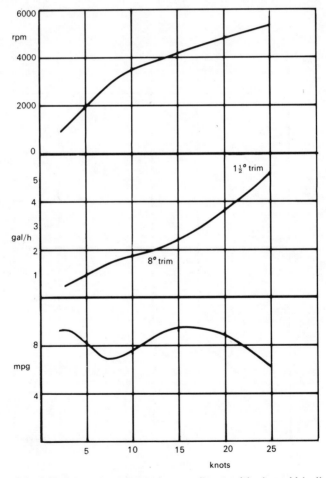

16-foot (5 m) Fletcher Arrowstreak speedboat with deep-V hull, in calm water. Trial weight 780 pounds (359 kg) plus two crew. Johnson 50 hp at 5500 rpm; 650 cc (41.5 cu. in.), two cylinders, loop charged, CD ignition, 2.42:1 reduction.

or those with not very powerful engines. The curve for the inflatable has a most peculiar double hump, and this appears in other tests on inflatables. As one might expect, the large flat wetted surface tends to be "draggy" at high speeds (over about 20 knots) and so despite their light weight they do not give

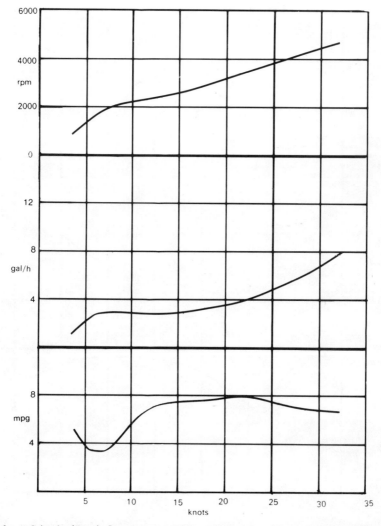

16-foot 6-inch (5 m) Sportsman 500 speedboat with gull-wing hull, in calm water. Trial weight 1270 pounds (570 kg) plus two persons. Chrysler 90 hp at 5000 rpm; 1186 cc (75 cu. in.), three cylinders, CD ignition, three carbs, 2:1 reduction.

such a good performance as a normal planing speedboat. For instance a 50-hp Johnson on a 14-foot inflatable gave 25 knots (46 km/hr) whereas the same engine on a 14-foot 6-inch chine speedboat gave 28½ knots (53 km/hr) despite the extra 450 pound (200 kg) weight. On the other hand, because of the large planing surface and low trim when just over the hump

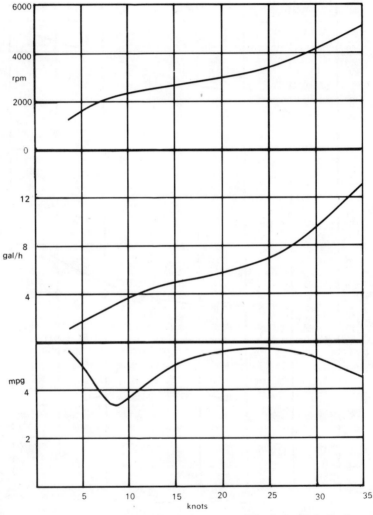

17-foot 4-inch (5.3 m) Chris-Craft Lancer with deep-V hull, in calm water. Trial weight 1600 pounds (735 kg) plus two persons. Evinrude 125 hp at 5000 rpm; 1632 cc (100 cu. in.), four cylinders, CD ignition, 2:1 reduction.

(the bows drop markedly when the hump is passed), inflatables are efficient at low planing speeds, say between 13 and 18 knots (24–33 km/hr). When heavily loaded they give good fuel consumption and lose less speed. The type of inflatable that has a rigid V-bottom gives a top-speed performance more akin to that of a normal speedboat.

Engine comparisons

The following tests enable comparisons to be made between different makes of motor of roughly the same nominal power, each run in turn on the back of the same boat (a 14-foot 6-inch (4.4 m) Neptune Smap with deep-V hull). In all cases the same load was used, the water was calm, and the best propeller and tilt angles were set for each motor to ensure a fair test. The graph sums up the results. The important particulars of the motors are:

	Cylinder capacity cc (cu. in.)	*Scavenging*	*No. of carbs*	*Reduction ratio*	*Prop size in. (mm)*
Chrysler 55	733 (45)	deflector on piston	1	1.62:1	$10\frac{3}{8} \times 13\frac{1}{2}$ (260 × 340)
Yamaha 55	760 (46)	flat-top piston	2	1.85:1	11×15 (280 × 380)
Mercury 50	718 (44)	direct charge	2	2.0:1	$11\frac{1}{4} \times 14$ (290 × 350)
Evinrude 50	680 (42)	loop charge	2	2.42:1	$12\frac{1}{4} \times 15$ (310 × 380)
Volvo 60	600 (37)	loop charge	3	2.67:1	$13\frac{3}{4} \times 15$ (350 × 380)

Comparing the curves with the particulars for each motor, some interesting trends show up. The top speeds achieved are roughly in proportion to the cylinder capacity and also to the full-throttle fuel consumption (i.e. greater capacity equals more speed and more fuel used) except for the Chrysler 55. However, at cruising speeds—and the best economical speed for this boat happens to be about 16 to 20 knots (30–37 km/hr)—variation in fuel consumption is very marked. Because the weight and trim of the boat was very similar with the different motors, the drag must have been very similar at any given speed. But one can see that in running at cruising speed the fuel consumed varied by a factor of up to two. By comparing the cylinder capacities it is clear that the motors with the greater capacity consumed more fuel. Whether this is the whole story is not clear because the low-capacity, economical motors also happen to be loop-charged, and also have a large reduction ratio and a greater number of carburetors. One would expect all these factors to have a bearing, but which one is most significant is not clear.

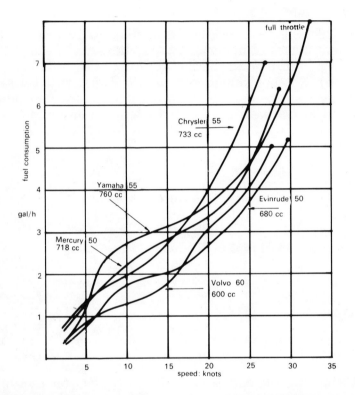

Comparative fuel consumptions in calm water of five different motors on the same boat, a 14-foot 6-inch (4.4 m) Neptune Smap with deep-V hull. Boat weight 660 pounds (300 kg) plus two crew.

The reduction ratio has some significance because the propeller slip at 19 knots, for instance, is: Chrysler 32 percent, Yamaha 30 percent, Mercury 25 percent, Evinrude 24 percent, Volvo 15 percent. The bigger the reduction ratio and therefore the bigger the propeller, the less the slip. More slip equals less efficiency and consequently more fuel consumed.

All these tests were conducted with a light load, and before

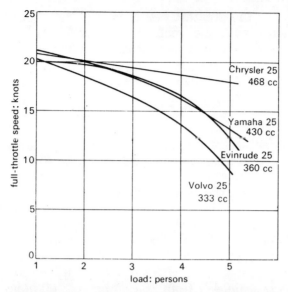

The effect of boat load on different outboards of the same horsepower in calm water. The bigger capacity motors keep the speed up. [Otter 440, 14-feet 7 inches (4.4 m), boat weight 430 pounds (196 kg).]

drawing further general conclusions it is worth looking at the effect of load, shown in the following tests.

In another series of tests a 14-foot 7-inch (4.4 m) Otter speed-boat was successively powered by four different motors of the same nominal horsepower and the top speeds measured with different loads. Speed dropped off with increasing load; the large-capacity motor kept the speed up, only losing about 3 knots (5.5 km/hr), while the smallest capacity motor lost about 11 knots (20 km/hr) and in fact the boat would not plane. Again the results show that the top speed with a light load is roughly in proportion to the cylinder size and fuel consumption. One could put it simply by saying that although the power at the top end is there irrespective of cylinder capacity etc., the torque at lower speeds depends very much on cylinder capacity.

To draw some conclusions, the top speed achieved is related to the cylinder capacity, and the greater the capacity the greater the full-throttle fuel consumption. This is the motor to choose if you want top speed. It is also the one for powering a heavy boat or towing skiers, or when the power chosen is close to the minimum for planing for the particular boat in mind. Another factor which helps in these conditions is a large reduction ratio and consequently a large propeller.

If you want the greatest fuel economy, then both tests indicate the motor with the smallest capacity for its horsepower, a large reduction ratio and loop or direct charging, with perhaps CD ignition and a carburetor per cylinder thrown in for good measure. The last two factors must also have a bearing on the top-speed performance.

The performance of the particular makes of motors mentioned do not necessarily reflect the character of all the motors in a manufacturer's range. If the technical details of one maker's range are examined it will often be found that some motors are out of step, as it were, usually because new models come along leaving the others behind.

A final point which should be mentioned again is that when choosing a motor size with a view to economy at the cruising speed, it is better to have a larger motor running slowly than a small motor which has to be run at nearly full throttle. This applies to speedboats which have motors in the lower half of the powering scale, say from $2\frac{1}{2}$ to 5 hp per 100 pounds (5.5 to 11 hp/100 kg), and is a good reason for choosing the next larger size of motor.

Towing skiers

The critical stage when pulling skiers is at low speeds when neither is the boat planing nor the skier up on the surface. A motor of high torque (for its horsepower) and a lower unit with a large reduction ratio and hence large propeller to grip the water are required. The first requirement is often satisfied by a relatively low-revving engine with a large cylinder capacity for its horsepower. A good skiing motor can be judged by its static thrust and acceleration from a standing start. The figures for the motors in the previously mentioned tests on 50- to 60-hp outboards are as follows:

	Cylinder capacity cc (cu. in.)	Reduction ratio	Prop. diam. in. (mm)	Static thrust lb. (kg)	Time over 100 m (328 ft.): standing start
Chrysler 55	733 (45)	1.62:1	10⅜ (260)	420 (190)	11.4
Yamaha 55	760 (46)	1.85:1	11 (280)	460 (210)	11.2
Mercury 50	718 (44)	2.0:1	11¼ (290)	430 (195)	11.4
Evinrude 50	680 (42)	2.42:1	12¼ (310)	530 (240)	10.4
Volvo 60	600 (37)	2.67:1	13¾ (350)	620 (280)	10.8

Since the bigger capacity motors happen to have small reduction ratios the two effects tend to cancel each other out, but nevertheless the effect of reduction ratio is clearly predominant, especially in the static thrust figures.

Propeller choice is also important if towing skiers is to be a regular job. A propeller suited for the boat alone will overload the motor when towing skiers. The revs at full throttle will never reach the manufacturers' maximum rev range and the engine will continuously labor. A propeller of lesser pitch is required, so that when towing the normal number of skiers the revs reach the correct mark. A rev counter is essential, as it is impossible to tell by ear alone whether the motor is overloaded or not. With a less pitched propeller, when the boat happens to run without skiers dangerous over-revving is possible and a rev counter at least gives a warning.

It is possible to ski using a 10-hp motor, but the boat must be small and light and of course only one light skier can be pulled. A 20-hp motor on boats up to about 13 feet will also tow one skier, but the bigger the motor (on a correspondingly bigger boat) the easier the pull-out, and the happier the skier.

Twin motor safety

A speedboat used on the sea or an estuary and powered by a single motor happens to be a type of boat that is prone to lead its owner into trouble. Outboards *do* let you down whatever the glossy brochures say, and even if you don't go more than

Two small twin outboards are more convenient in many kinds of boating, and safer in most. In some situations, only one of the outboards need be used. The second should then be raised to reduce drag.

half a mile or so offshore a breakdown can (and does) rapidly spiral into serious trouble. A speedboat wallowing around and drifting in a choppy sea is vulnerable: its freeboard and static stability are relatively low, its weight is concentrated at the stern, especially if one or two people are working over the motor, and what may have started out as a happy burn-up soon becomes a frightening experience in a worsening sea. The wise owner therefore runs in company with another boat, and takes the following equipment: a spare can of fuel (and some outboard oil), elementary tools, sparkplugs and a plug wrench, shear pins, lifejackets, an anchor and long warp (rope), a bilge pump (or a bucket), flares, a small compass (for sudden mist or fog) and a small fire extinguisher.

It is sensible to carry a small get-you-home outboard. A pair of oars and rowlocks for emergency propulsion is a quite feasible proposition on some speedboats. Paddles are of dubious use, especially up-wind, but better than nothing if there are two of them.

A more elegant solution to the problem of reliability is to fit twin motors. This also brings other advantages. Where one has to travel for some distance in a speed-restricted area before arriving at open water, running on one engine (with the other tilted up to avoid drag) will return a much better fuel consumption than running one larger engine slowly. The initial cost of two motors is higher, but mounting and demounting two 30-hp motors rather than one 60-hp weighing perhaps 200 pounds (90 kg) is very much easier. Twin motors make the boat so much more flexible in use. A rigid tie-bar should be fitted between the two motors for common steering, making sure first that the motors are aligned parallel. To obviate torque reaction one cannot fit a propeller of opposite hand on one motor and run that motor in reverse, because the gear is not generally designed for continuous high-speed running in reverse.

The performance given by twin motors of the same nominal total horsepower as one large motor is roughly equal, as the following figures show.

Top speed

	One person knots (km/hr)	Two persons knots (km/hr)
14-foot runabout		
one 40-hp Johnson	26.3 (48)	21.6 (40)
two 18-hp Johnsons	23.7 (43)	21.5 (40)
16-foot runabout		
one 35-hp Perkins	26.2 (48)	24.7 (45)
two 16-hp Perkins	25.9 (47)	24.5 (45)

Another illuminating test concerned two identical inflatable boats (17-foot 6-inch Zodiac MK IV), one powered by a 50-hp Johnson and the other by two 25-hp Johnsons. The top speeds were 24.4 knots (45 km/hr) and 22.7 knots (42 km/hr) respectively. The two craft were run in company over a distance of 135 miles (250 km), mostly at high speed. The average fuel consumptions were 6.9 mpg (2.8 km/L) for 50 hp and 3.9 mpg (1.6 km/L) for the twin 25s, which may seem to contradict my earlier statement, but this test was carried out at high speeds at around three-quarter throttle or more. It is a fact that large motors consume less fuel for each horsepower produced than small motors, so one would expect that the 50-hp motor giving out say 40-hp would consume less than the twins also giving a total of 40-hp. But at lower speeds the situation reverses. A big motor will be running at a very small fraction of its full power and be more thirsty for each horsepower produced than one 25-hp motor, which will be working relatively harder and consequently more economically to produce the same boat speed. The conclusion to be drawn is that if most of your running will be at high speeds then twins will be more thirsty. But if a good proportion of the time will be spent running at low throttle (where one motor can be switched off), then twins will save on fuel.

At high speeds, a single large outboard drinks less fuel than twin engines.

Outboards for Sailboats

A small outboard is commonly used for auxiliary propulsion on small sailing dayboats and cruisers. It interferes very little with the boat as a sailing machine in terms of weight, space and propeller drag (as it can be tilted or raised out of the water when sailing). If a motor is only required to push the boat out of a harbor or a marina and as a get-you-home device in flat calms, the outboard approaches the ideal. But if propulsion is required in choppy water and strong winds, and particularly if the boat is 20 feet or more in length, problems start to arise. In such conditions the power required to maintain speed doubles or trebles; but apart from this, a motor perched right aft on the transom of a pitching yacht can hardly be expected to give much push if the propeller is constantly coming out of the water. Size of motor, mounting position and shaft length are therefore factors which need some thought. Another point to consider is that for cruising or evening sailing, electricity is very convenient for running and cabin lights, in which case an outboard fitted with a suitable generator is required.

Before getting down to these problems the pros and cons of outboard versus inboard motors should be mentioned. If the comparison is to be made on equal performance (i.e. effective propulsion) under power, it is necessary to take an outboard of higher nominal power than an inboard, for three reasons. The nominal power of an outboard is usually a sprint rating measured at the crankshaft rather than a continuous rating at the gearbox coupling, as is the case for most inboards. The smaller propeller of an outboard gives less basic propulsive efficiency, and in rough water is more affected by pitching and wave action.

So let us consider a 5-hp inboard and an 8- to 10-hp outboard.

With this set-up, both outboard and mount are removed and stowed when under sail. The outboard is fixed; boat is steered with its own rudder.

The weight of the outboard will be around 50 pounds (23 kg) compared to several hundred pounds for an inboard, particularly when the weight of its installation and sterngear is taken into account. The extra weight of an inboard engine does not tend to improve the ballast ratio of the yacht because it is generally situated somewhere near the center of gravity of the bare boat and certainly not at the bottom of the keel. Consequently sailing performance suffers. The cost of a bare inboard engine is considerably more than that of an outboard, and again one must take installation costs into account. Another disadvantage of the inboard is that it takes up space within the boat, and is usually much more difficult to work on in its confined compartment, and far harder to take ashore.

Inboards are more reliable, particularly diesels, and more convenient to use (no leaning over the transom to tilt and rope-start the outboard). They are not liable to be swamped, cannot be stolen or dropped in the water, and give more effective propulsion. There are also advantages in electricity generation and fuel consumption. If much motoring is envisaged, fuel costs for an outboard become considerable, though perhaps not

The outboard on this sailing dinghy is designed for auxiliary use, and has an extra long shaft. Rewave of shorts shafts: they are prone to ventilation.

decisive if one stops to consider the money saved in choosing outboard propulsion in the first place. Finally, an outboard stuck on an ungainly bracket on the transom is rather unsightly, and some people feel that it spoils the overall looks of their boat.

Many small fiberglass sailing boats are designed from the outset for outboard propulsion and the interior moldings (and often hull shape) preclude the installation of an inboard. As size increases so too does the pitching problem, while the increasing weight of the required size of outboard makes man-handling it more difficult. Consequently, larger sailing boats tend to be inboard powered. The crossover occurs at around 20 feet (6 m), but it also depends on whether the motor is intended for serious propulsion in terms of hours and rough water, or just for getting in and out of harbor.

Choice of motor

In choosing a make there are the usual all-important questions of spares and service facilities, then what power is suitable and what features make a good auxiliary. Broadly speaking, one wants a quiet, reliable motor with a good reduction ratio and a really long shaft; also a lock to the satisfaction of the insurance surveyor, and if necessary a generator. Such a motor does not exist. Some have longer shafts than the standard 20 in (500 mm) long-shaft, some are quiet, a few have generators—but there is no one motor that satisfies on all counts. The standard transom heights of 15 inches (380 mm) and 20 inches (500 mm) for all motors irrespective of power come from the requirements of the speedboat world, but even 20 inches (500 mm) is far too low a shaft length for a yacht say 25 feet long. The permissible rise and fall of the water surface relative to the motor can only be roughly 10 inches (250 mm) upwards before the engine is in danger of being swamped, and 10 inches (250 mm) downwards before the propeller starts thrashing in the air. Hulls differ in their behavior: some rise late to a wave, others are very buoyant. Of course as the water level rises so too does the boat, so a wave 20 inches (500 mm) high does not by any means reduce the motor's effectiveness to nil, but the importance of shaft length is obvious, especially as the boat's size increases. For

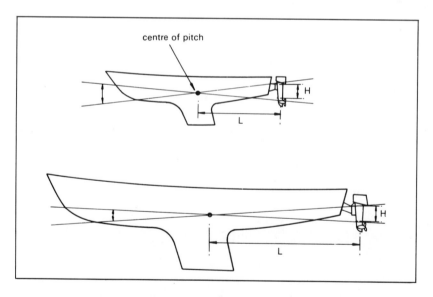

Because the transom height H is constant regardless of the size of the motor, the larger the yacht, the less the permissible pitch angle befor the outboard is in danger of being swamped or the propeller of coming out of the water. With transom stern motorboats the center of pitch is farther aft and the outboard closer to the transom, so the distance L is less. An inboard trunk arrangement also reduces the length L.

most makes the longest is the standard long-shaft of 20 inches (500 mm). Sometimes the smallest motors in a maker's range can be extended with a special kit, and one or two makes have a good length of shaft (Seagull or Mariner, for instance). Besides ensuring that the propeller is deeply immersed and the motor head high enough to avoid being swamped, it is much more convenient to have the controls and starter grip showing and easily accessible above the top of the transom.

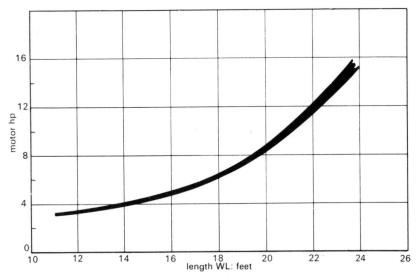

Sensible outboard motor size for sailing boats, giving adequate performance in reasonably calm conditions.

A motor with a large reduction ratio will give significantly greater thrust at the speeds that a sailing yacht is likely to achieve under power (around 5 knots or 9 km/hr). A large reduction ratio enables a large and slow-revving propeller to be used. For outboards whose engines revolve at 4000 to 5000 rpm a reduction of 1.5:1 can be considered poor, 2.5:1 good, and 3.5:1 very good. These figures give a practical guide when choosing a motor. In fact, to swing a propeller of the same di-

The particular outboard at right, the Chrysler 150 Sailor, was made to suit the power needs of larger cruising sailboats not fitted with an inboard engine, or to serve as an emergency get-home engine on power cruisers.

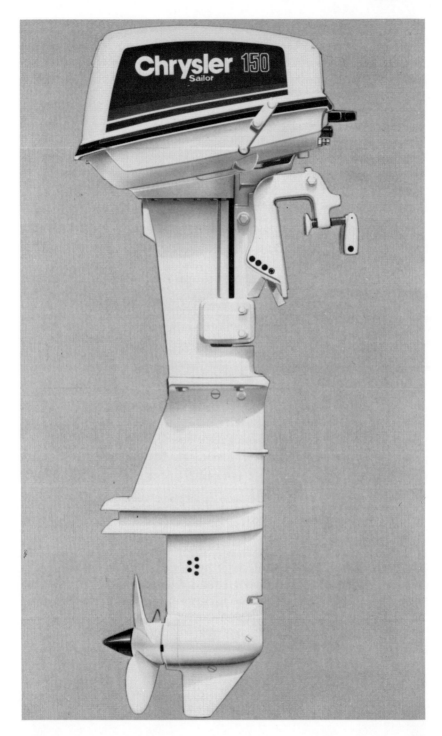

ameter as that used with an average small inboard engine, the reduction ratio would have to be about 4 : 1.

What power to choose? The graph can be used as a guide for conventional outboards, and a speed in calm water of about 5 knots (9 km/hr) can be expected. But the larger the size of boat the greater the drop in propulsive efficiency that can be expected in rougher conditions. From the point of view of initial cost and portability the smaller the motor the better, but it is inadvisable to go below the line unless the motor has a particularly good (high) reduction ratio.

Mounting

There are several ways of mounting an outboard on a sailing cruiser. A motor boat type transom is one way, and the requirements of transom height and self-bailing wells are the same as those described in the previous chapter on speedboats. If the cockpit is self-bailing there is really no need for a well. On a small open dayboat a long-shaft outboard may simply fit on the transom without the need for a cut-out, or in a bracket. Many boats have an after deck and consequently a bolted-on bracket or a trunk is necessary.

Problems with the bracket arrangement occur if the transom is sharply raked, very narrow, or if there is a transom-hung rudder. A fixed bracket has to protrude farther out from the transom if the motor is to be able to tilt—21½ inches (550 mm) to be precise. On larger boats even a long-shaft motor may disappear below the top of the transom, making starting and controlling it very difficult. The way out of many of these problems is to use a swinging or sliding bracket so that in the up position the head is accessible for starting and the leg out of the water for sailing, and in the down position the propeller is well immersed for driving. It also avoids having to allow the motor space to tilt, and consequently it can be hung closer to the transom.

Ready-made fixed, swinging and sliding brackets are available, and one or two outboard manufacturers list brackets as accessories. Making a bracket is a relatively simple do-it-yourself job. Sturdiness is the keynote, plus careful consideration of the geometry of the whole bearing in mind tilting and height requirements. As always, the propeller should see clear water ahead of it and not be partially masked by the transom. The motor should also sit vertically. The top of the mounting bracket should be between 6 and 13 inches (150–330 mm) above the static waterline for a short-shaft motor, and 11–18 inches

(280–450 mm) in the case of a long-shaft. Or to put it another way, the cavitation plate should be 2 to 9 inches (50–230 mm) below the surface. There is the compromise between propeller emergence and motor swamping to consider; and bear in mind that the more the motor is mounted off the centerline the more it will seesaw when the boat rolls, which is in addition to the fore-and-aft movement of pitching.

Having got the geometry right (making a scale drawing is best), mild steel tube, angle bar or flat bar can be used to make the bracket. Welded joints can be made by a local garage or small metal-working firm. It is best to pre-cut everything to size and prepare the joints and clamp them together so that the welder can get straight on with his job. A few different do-it-yourself bracket arrangements are shown in; all of them have

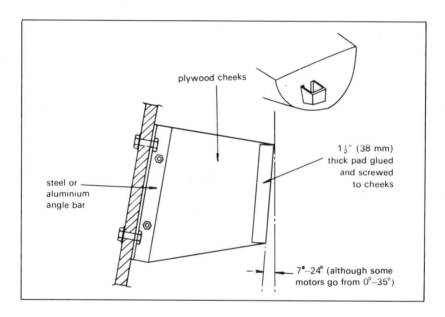

plywood cheeks

steel or aluminium angle bar

1½″ (38 mm) thick pad glued and screwed to cheeks

7°–24° (although some motors go from 0°–35°)

A simple fixed transom bracket for small outboards. The required area of pad and the distance off the transom can be found in previous graphs.

been made and do work. A bracket made of mild steel is strong and rigid and is best protected by hot-dip galvanizing; otherwise an epoxy or two-part polyurethane paint over primer is next best. A sliding bracket is more difficult to make and align on the boat, and also tends to jam. In all cases a positive means must be provided to hold the motor up: if it fell down it might wrench the

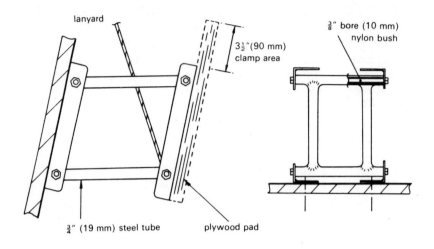

lanyard

$3\frac{1}{2}$"(90 mm) clamp area

$\frac{3}{8}$" bore (10 mm) nylon bush

$\frac{3}{4}$" (19 mm) steel tube   plywood pad

A swinging motor bracket suitable for the Seagull bracket, or, with a plywood pad, for normal clamp mounting.

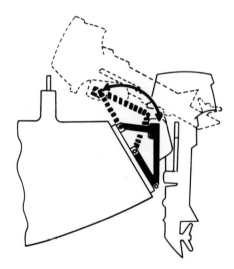

Another bracket on a 20-footer which makes for easy access to the power head or prop from the cockpit. The bracket is built from steel angle and flat bar; a mock-up should first be made to establish the correct length of the link arms.

bolts through the transom. A lanyard and cleat is one simple way, or a locking pin or strut on the bracket itself. An elegant solution is to counterbalance the weight of the motor by a built-in spring which then also takes out part of the effort in hauling up the motor. (The Bremer bracket has this arrangement.) It is advisable to reinforce the transom under the heads or nuts of all the holding-on bolts to spread the load; a thick plywood pad is suitable. If the boat has a pointed or very steeply raked stern, or is a multihull, then a side bracket is probably the best answer, being specially made to suit the geometry.

It is usually better to fix the motor in the fore-and-aft position and steer by using the boat's rudder, although it may be that the turning circle is rather large in which case it may be better to steer with the motor in congested waters. A transom-hung rudder may require a stop, or simply a lanyard on the tiller when under power. Mounting the outboard off the centerline does not normally affect steering to any noticeable degree.

A trunk built into the boat is a better way of mounting an outboard with regard to looks and pitching. It comes much closer to an inboard installation, and the propeller is covered by the hull's surface and nearer to the boat's center of pitch. How-

Using the rudder in this configuration is difficult. The young boatmen have opted to lash the tiller and steer by means of the outboard.

ever, unless the trunk is very large the motor cannot tilt. In most cases the keel or bilge keels will protect the motor when accidentally running aground, but it is a point to bear in mind on centerboard boats. A sliding bracket inside the trunk allows the motor to be lifted clear of the water when sailing or on moorings. The hole in the hull creates drag when sailing, but a flush cover or plug can be arranged in some cases. Exhaust fumes invading the cockpit can be a problem with trunks, depending on whether the exhaust is under water or not, and on how the trunk is ventilated. Ventilation is usually vital if the motor is not to choke on its own fumes, and exhaust that circulates round the cockpit or cabin can be sick-making or dangerous. For motors of up to 12 hp the following is the absolute minimum trunk size: width 18 inches (460 mm), length 26 inches (660 mm). The clear height above the top of transom (i.e. the place on which the bracket clamps) must be at least 19 inches (480 mm), and the hole in the bottom of the boat 9 inches (230 mm) wide by about 12 inches (300 mm) long.

Catamarans

A motor on each hull, or one motor on the centerline projecting through the bridge deck into the water? In some ways a center motor is more vulnerable to pitching and sheer wave action. Two motors cost much more than one of the same total power, and it is more normal to find a single center motor mounted on the transom or projecting through a hole in the deck or through a short trunk. Water tends to fountain-up through a hole in the deck, so a trunk with a lid on it has advantages especially as the noise can then be shut out. Slim-hulled catamarans or trimarans of light displacement for their length have an inherently greater speed potential under sail *or* power than monohulls, so it is possible to employ an overlarge motor and expect speeds higher than the normal limit of 6 to 7 knots (11 to 13 km/hr). But the majority of *cruising* catamarans (and tris) are heavy and have hulls which are "draggy," so potential speeds under power are little better than for a monohull of the same waterline length.

The following test results on a cruising cat are therefore roughly representative of the performance of a monohull of the same waterline length and similarly powered. Three long-shaft Chrysler outboards of 6, 12.9 and 20 hp were tested on a 22-foot (6.7 m) Hirondelle catamaran. The pertinent features of these motors are:

Hp	Weight lb. (kg)	Reduction ratio	Propeller diam. × pitch in. (mm)	Capacity cc (cu. in.)
6	47 (21)	1.53:1	8 × 5 (204 × 127)	147 (8.99)
12.9	59 (27)	1.57:1	8¼ × 6 (210 × 152)	222 (13.62)
20	79 (36)	1.5:1	8½ × 6 (215 × 152)	330 (19.96)

All the motors were twin-cylinder, water-cooled, with magneto ignition, and ran on 50:1 mixture and had reverse gears.

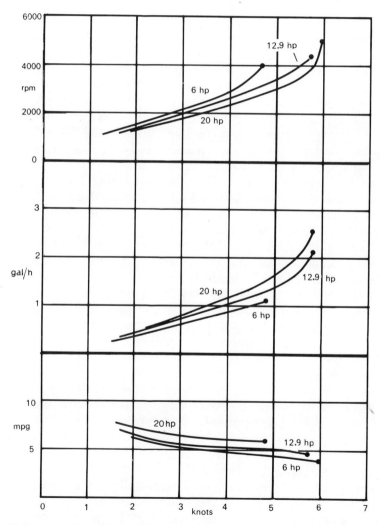

Performance of a 22-foot (6.8 m) cruising catamaran powered by three different Chrysler outboards in calm water.

The two larger units had electric starting and charging. The tests were carried out in calm water, the top speeds being:

6 hp	4.8 knots	(8.9 km/hr)
12.9 hp	5.8 knots	(10.7 km/hr)
20 hp	5.9 knots	(11 km/hr)

The fact that there is so little difference between the speeds with the 20-hp and 12.9-hp motors is due to two things. First, the resistance of any boat begins to rise very sharply at a speed of around 1.3 × the square root of the waterline length in feet. For the Hirondelle cat this equals 5.8 knots. Second, the 12.9-hp motor appears to be more powerful than its nominal rating suggests. The propeller sizes of the two motors are virtually identical, while the full-throttle propeller revs in the case of the 20-hp engine are only slightly greater. The propeller of the 20-hp motor also suffers from excessive slip at high throttle openings because of its small size, and this can be seen by the curling-up of the rpm lines at the top end. Wide-blade propellers are available for some Chrysler engines, and these are worthwhile for slower boats to reduce cavitation and slip. The most cost-effective motor for all-round performance was the 12.9-hp although the 20-hp was quieter. The 6-hp was adequate for calm water, but its effectiveness would drop considerably in choppy conditions or against a moderate headwind. These motors are modern, quiet, smooth and well waterproofed, but suffer from their low reduction ratio when asked to push displacement boats along. One consequence is that fuel mileage achieved is a little lower than normal. The best mpg consistent with reasonably fast progress is achieved at a speed (in knots) corresponding roughly to the square root of the waterline length (in feet), and this rule applies to any displacement boat, whether cruising cat, monohull or motor boat. For a boat 20 feet on the waterline this means 4½ knots; 25 feet, 5 knots; and so on. Working in meters and km/hr, take the square root of the WL length and multiply by 3½. Forcing a boat to go faster rapidly diminishes the miles covered on a gallon of fuel. Notice too that the results show that a bigger motor is thirstier than a smaller one when propelling the boat at a particular speed.

To get the best performance out of a small motor pushing a yacht, whether a multihull or a monohull, it is essential to fit the propeller which allows the motor to rev up to its full rated rpm. Several horsepower can be lost by a too-large propeller, and when there are not many horses available the loss is very noticeable. It is a once-only exercise to check the rpm, so a rev

The prop driving a sailing yacht should allow the engine to reach its full rated rpm. Wide blades are better here, and three blades better than two.

counter need only be borrowed. Usually the propeller which will allow the full revs to be developed is the finest-pitched one available from the motor manufacturers. If there is a suitable wide-blade choice, take it; also take three blades in preference to two. There is normally no point in paying more money for a propeller other than the standard aluminum variety. Correct size is more important than the material.

If a motor is to be stowed inboard, under a cockpit seat for example, it should lie so that the head is above the level of the lower unit, to prevent water in the exhaust pipe running back up into the cylinder. This is best achieved by arranging a bar on to which the motor can be clamped. It is also desirable to drain the carburetor via the stopcock (if fitted) to avoid dripping fuel. If there is an integral tank make sure the tap is off and the filler end of the tank uppermost.

Inland Boating Tips

Lakes, inland waterways, canals and non-tidal rivers pose several problems to outboard users. On shallow waterways, the propeller is liable to hit obstructions on the bottom and pick up weed and plastic bags. Because speeds are often restricted by law or by the physical limitation of water depth, motors are required to run slowly-for long periods. The wash must not upset other people in boats moored to the bank, nor erode the banks. Acceptable speeds on the narrow British canals work out at 3 or at the most 4 knots ($5\frac{1}{2}$ to $7\frac{1}{2}$ km/hr), river speeds 4 to 5 knots ($7\frac{1}{2}$ to 9 km/hr). The actual developed power required is thus very low, consequently even a small outboard may only produce, when cruising normally, a fraction of its full-throttle horsepower (which leaves a significant reserve for the rougher conditions found on lakes and large rivers). This kind of use leads to repeated sparkplug fouling, excessive fuel consumption, poor starting, and low or non-existent charging current. Two-stroke engines perform inefficiently at low throttle openings; the fuel/air mixture is not fully burned, hence the carbon formation on the plugs. Some motors which have electric starting and charging do not actually start charging until quite high revs are reached, and the boat is then going excessively fast for restricted running.

Overpowering

Choosing the correct size of outboard much reduces these problems. Too often inland craft are overpowered: unlike the sea situation, there is often no need for a large margin of power for bad weather or a foul tide, and little more than the calm water power making 4 to 5 knots is generally required. To illustrate just how small is this minimum power, consider the following test results on a 17-foot 6-inch fiberglass cabin cruiser (a Shetland Family Four) and on a 24-foot canal cruiser (Dobson 24). The curves (25) show how trivial is the drag or towrope pull: at 3 knots the drag is only 25 pounds (11 kg) for the small boat and 30 pounds (14 kg) for the larger. At 4 knots the figures are 45 and 70 pounds (20 and 32 kg). A child could probably manage to pull either boat along at 4 knots (7.4 km/hr). The actual towrope horsepowers required to produce these speeds are labelled on the curves and these are correspondingly trivial. When these boats are pushed along by a propeller there is inevitable inefficiency due to propeller slip; in fact about half the power delivered to the propeller is wasted. So to put it another way, the power delivered by the engine to the propeller is about twice that of the towrope horsepower.

In the tests, these two boats were pushed along by a 15-hp motor in the case of the small 17-footer and a 6-hp motor in the case of the 24-footer. At 3 knots (5.5 km/hr) the 15-hp motor

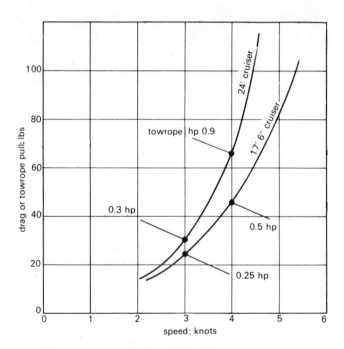

The pull needed to tow two typical canal cruisers (17-foot and 24-foot) through still water. An outboard pushing these boats along has to overcome this resistance, which at very slow speeds is trivial.

Planing hulls leave little wake when on plane—the largest wake is generated at the hump. But safety dictates both slow speeds and no wake in narrow channels.

was actually developing about 0.5 hp, and at 4 knots (7.4 km/hr) about 1 hp, while the 6-hp motor was developing about 0.6 and about 1.8 hp respectively. Clearly at canal speeds they are working extremely lightly at a fraction of their full power. No wonder they tend to foul their plugs. But in the case of the 6-hp motor the tendency is considerably less marked.

Another aspect is that the drags and horsepowers involved are much the same for both boats despite the large discrepancy in size. The Shetland weighed, at the time, less than ¾ ton (750 kg) while the Dobson weighed about 1½ tons (1500 kg). This is a matter of hydrodynamics; at these low speds weight is not very significant. Length on the waterline is the more important criteria, and the extra length of the Dobson 24 made up for her extra weight. Another point is that the *small* motor propelled the large boat, yet its power was adequate for stopping the boat, maneuvering in locks and coping with gusts of wind. In other words, the 15-hp motor on the Shetland was too powerful for the size of boat for canal work; it would be adequate for big lakes, estuaries or even coastal cruising.

Overpowering also causes excessive fuel consumption. To see the effect on fuel consumption of using different sizes of outboards, it is necessary to take a single boat and power it with different sizes of motors. The curves show typical real consumptions achieved on test, and it is very clear that the larger the outboard the greater the fuel consumption at a given slow speed. One curve is labelled 70 to 100 hp, which is of course a ridiculous size of motor for a small inland cruiser (or a large inland cruiser for that matter), and even 20- and 40-hp motors are too large for the very restricted conditions of canal use. These powers are shown for academic interest. Choosing a 6- or 10-hp motor can more than halve the fuel consumption at 3 or 4 knots: not only are fuel costs less but the initial cost of the motor is less.

That I say a 20-hp motor is too large for a 20-footer for slow river or canal cruising may be surprising in view of the large

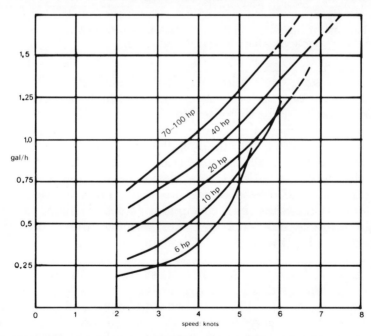

Typical relative fuel consumptions of different sized outboards powering small inland cruisers in the 17- to 22-foot range.

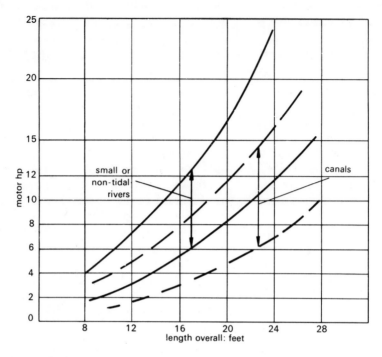

Sensible motor sizes for canals and rivers where there are no strong currents or winds, or where speed is restricted.

number of such boats afloat with this size of motor. One particular owner of a 20-foot cruiser with a 20-hp motor chose the electric start version in order to charge a battery for cabin lights. He also chose the 20-hp motor on the advice of the boat dealer, who said that the stopping power and general maneuvering would be better. This is quite true, of course, but the penalty was that to cruise within the regulation canal speed the motor only turned at 2000 to 3000 rpm, producing a tiny fraction of its full 20-hp. Consequently it continually fouled its plugs, causing rough running and stoppages. Furthermore, the motor consumed a gallon every three miles, and was not running fast enough for the generator to cut in and charge the battery. Naturally the owner was rather upset that his motor was not doing the intended job. There were several ways out of the problem: change to a 10-hp electric start motor and lose money on the deal; fit a tiny propeller and let the motor buzz away giving little thrust and speed; increase the drag of the boat by ballasting; buy a few sets of hot plugs and carry a portable generator to charge the battery. A 5- or 10-hp motor would have been working harder to give the same boat speed; its fuel consumption would have been far lower; and as the revs would have been higher the generator would have produced net charging current.

Having stressed the evils of overpowering, there are real dangers in underpowering, such as poor handling in windy conditions or against strong current. A boat with little draft and high sides and superstructure will require a larger motor for control than an open launch with a good deep keel and a low profile above water. For boats around 20 feet, a 5-hp motor represents the bottom end of the sensible scale for sheltered use, and about 12-hp the upper end, depending on windage rather than weight. It is with these factors in mind that the graph is shown as a guide to choosing suitable power. Whereas canals and small inland lakes usually mean still water, rivers can mean strong currents, choppy waves, and exposure to windy conditions.

On larger lakes or wide, deep non-tidal rivers a few extra horsepower can sensibly be used to gain more speed; rivers also tend to be a little more exposed, and in times of flood the current can run very fast. Wind on lakes can be very strong indeed, and build up so quickly that it is impossible to avoid it.

Among the conventional two-strokes the best outboard for such inland cruising is the one that will not soot-up at low revs, and here surface gap plugs, electronic ignition and 50:1 fuel mixtures make their contribution. With side-electrode plugs, fitting hotter plugs than normally recommended often helps a great deal to prevent sooting-up. Ideally a motor should be air cooled to give freedom from blocked intakes and scored water pump housings (common troubles in shallow, debris-laden water), but air-cooled motors are generally noisier and quietness is something that is very desirable on tranquil waters.

In all cases where expected boat speeds are low, a large reduction ratio is desirable, but this is not quite so essential in the case of cruisers as in the situation where a displacement boat is being driven at the maximum hull speed, producing large waves and wash. At 3 or 4 knots ($5\frac{1}{2}$ to $7\frac{1}{2}$ km/hr) any boat more than about 16-feet long slips through the water with hardly a ripple and the thrust required is small. Nevertheless 2:1 reduction is far preferable to 1.5:1, and the stopping power (if it's important) will be correspondingly greater. A small motor with 3:1 reduction will be the equal of a larger motor with 1.5:1.

It is interesting to compare the performance of an outboard with that of a diesel at these very slow speeds. Unlike a two-stroke gasoline engine, a diesel maintains its efficient combustion down to quite low revs, and consequently compared to an outboard becomes more and more economical as the throttle is closed. In a test of two Dobson 24-foot cruisers, one powered by a 6-hp diesel inboard and the other by a 6-hp outboard, the fuel consumption of the diesel at full throttle was half that of the outboard. As diesel is also the cheaper fuel, this was a marked economy, but the gap became wider at slower speeds until at 3½ knots (6½ km/hr) the diesel consumed 1.2 pints (0.57 L) every hour compared to 4.2 pints (2 L) every hour for the outboard. Hence the respective mpg figures were 34 and 10 (11.4 and 3.2 km/hr). Imagine the difference if the outboard boat had been overpowered! An incidental feature was that although the nominal horsepowers were the same, the diesel boat had another ½ knot (1 km/hr) of top speed, and in a tug-of-war towed the outboard boat had another ½ knot (1 km/hr) of top speed, and in a tug-of-war towed the outboard boat backwards at about 2 knots (3½ km/hr). This was partly because of the diesel's larger and slower turning propeller: 15½-inch (390 mm) diameter at 937 rpm as against 8-inch (200 mm) at 2600 rpm. Its maneuvering and stopping power was similarly greater.

Props don't last long when run carelessly in shallow lakes and rivers. Inspect the prop for damage, and keep a replacement on hand. Here, a weedless prop could be used.

Against these benefits were much greater initial costs and more vibration and noise.

A four-stroke inboard gasoline engine would come, in performance and cost, somewhere in between the diesel inboard and the two-stroke outboard. Similarly, a four-stroke outboard would burn fuel much more efficiently at low revs, giving good fuel consumption and little plug fouling. So again, one sees the unfulfilled need for a quiet and smooth four-stroke outboard with a large reduction ratio.

Generators

The smaller outboards on the market often do not have the option of electric starting and charging. Exceptions include the Johnson and Evinrude 10 and 15 hp, Chrysler 10, 15 and 20 hp, Mercury 20 hp, Ocean, Selva 20 and Archimedes 9 and 14-hp. Some of these can be converted by fitting an electric start kit. Other small non-electric start motors have a flywheel generator incorporated as a standard fitting; some can be adapted with a battery charging kit. There are two important things to determine before one buys an electric start or battery charging version of an outboard: will the charger cut in at *normal* cruising revs, and will the current delivered at these revs be sufficient? On some motors the generator does not cut in and commence charging until the revs are quite high, and this may be inherent in the design of the generator.

The current output of most generators on outboards is usually quite small. For instance, Johnson 10- and 15-hp electric start motors give 2 amps (24 watts) at 2000 rpm rising to 5 amps (60 watts) at 4000 rpm. The Chrysler 10- and 15-hp auto-electrics give 10 amps (120 watts) at 3800 rpm. The Mercury 10- and 7½-hp motors can have a coil generator giving 10 watts (watts = amps × volts, and many systems are 12 volt). The Yamaha 8, 12, 15 and 20 have 40 watt coils, and the Archimedes motors range between 17 and 60 watts output. Normally the wattage quoted is the maximum developed only at high revs.

Current output must be equated with the current consumed, otherwise the battery will gradually be discharged and will have to be taken ashore and recharged every so often. Suppose the only load on the battery was cabin lights of a total of 24 watts. If they are switched on in the evening for, say, three hours they will consume 2 amps (12 volt system) so the amount of electricity consumed is 6 amp hours (amps × hours). Batteries of at least 30 amp hours (AH) are usually specified, so there is no fear of running a *fully* charged battery flat during an evening. But will the generator be able to replace the electricity during the next day's running? If the motor runs for the same number of hours as the lights were on, the output will have to be 24 watts (plus a little for battery inefficiency); if it runs for only 1½ hours the output must be 48 watts, and so on. You may want to run navigation lights, a bilge pump or even a television set, so the output of the generator must be greater still at *cruising* revs in order to even up the score. It should not be necessary to put in a full day's running to make up for the previous night's electricity consumption: you may not want to go that far, or you may want to stay and enjoy a pleasant spot. It is clear that the generator output can be critical and one must economize on the use of electricity on board, and even be prepared to take the battery home occasionally and charge it up overnight. With electric starting the load on the battery is of course even greater, probably the next day after it's run down. In the event of a flat battery most electric start outboards are fitted with a manual recoil starter, so there is no fear of getting stuck.

Weed

So-called "weedless" propellers available for some of the smaller outboards have blades skewed away from the direction of rotation as they curve out to the tips, so that weed tends to be thrown off by centrifugal force rather than trapped in the hollow by the boss. While not truly weedless, they are less prone to catching weed. A wire cage around the propeller is another solution, which also prevents the blades being worn away by frequent churning in mud and stones. However the drag of a cage made of close wire mesh considerably affects the performance. The standard aluminum propellers tend to chip and erode rather easily, so it might be worth considering the much more expensive bronze or stainless steel versions if they are available for the small motor. Plastic propellers are claimed to be a little more durable than aluminum ones, but cost much the same, and are available for several smaller motors.

On many inland cruisers there is no keel or skeg to protect the lower leg projecting below the bottom of the transom, so the motor must be able to tilt up quite freely. This is a point to bear in mind if the motor is mounted on a bracket close to the transom. In any case, even in fresh water it is very desirable to be able to tilt the leg out of the water when the motor is not in use, and to be able to free weed and debris from the propeller. A tubular steel guard mounted off the transom can give

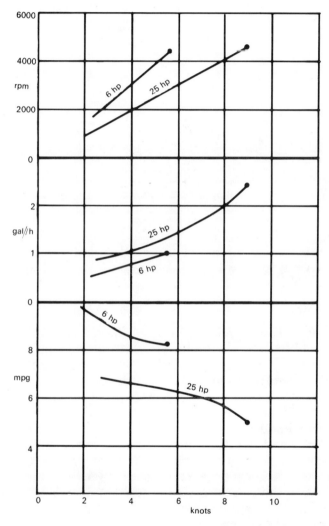

Peformance of a typical 20-foot (6 m) fiberglass inland cruiser (Sunspeed) with a shallow chine hull, powered by two different Johnson outboards. Trial weight 2000 pounds (900 kg). Two-cylinder engines running on 50:1 mixture; 145 cc (8.8 cu. in.) with 1.72:1 reduction, and 360 cc (22 cu. in.) with 1.75:1. The 25-hp motor is too large for inland use and the 6-hp a trifle too small.

The outboard on this small bass boat is probably too large. Overpowering causes the prop to slip, losing efficiency and wasting fuel.

some protection to the motor in crowded moorings, but again it must allow it to tilt up.

Propeller size

As in other kinds of boating, it is most important to fit a size of propeller that allows the motor at full throttle to rev up to the rpm range specified by the manufacturers. Not that full-throttle operation is ever required, but this ensures that the motor is not laboring at lower revs from a too-large propeller. This situation causes much trouble from plug fouling. On the other hand a propeller that only allows the revs to reach the bottom end of the specified range rather than the top, tends to give a slightly better fuel consumption when cruising. The only way to check whether the correct propeller is fitted is to install or borrow a tachometer. In most cases the correct propeller will be the smallest-pitched one listed in the manufacturer's range for your particular outboard model.

Steering

Many outboard boats powered for low speeds have poor steering qualities. On a supposedly straight course their lack of keel and rudder and their shallow draft make them directionally unstable, and the high sides tend to catch the wind. The course actually steered is a continual zigzag and maneuvering becomes a rather hit-and-miss affair. There are two ways to improve matters; first, by fitting a rudder on to the lower unit of the outboard, abaft the propeller. There are several makes of such rudders specifically intended for outboards and they are not very expensive. A rudder makes the boat more directionally stable and the steering at very low speeds—when approaching a jetty for instance— more positive. But it does not help the windage problem. The more basic cure is to fit a long keel to the hull, sloping deeper as it goes aft. On a typical small shallow draft 20-foot hard-chine fiberglass cruiser, a keel at least 1 foot (30 cm) deep at its after end is required. Ballast also helps to slow down the reaction to wind, and generally creates inertia. On a 20-footer at least 300 to 450 pounds (150 to 200 kg) is necessary to make a noticeable difference, i.e. about 15 to 20 percent of the all-up weight of the boat.

A rudder is fairly easy to make from $\frac{1}{8}$-inch (3 mm) thick aluminum plate with square-section tube (or less preferably, angle bar) bolted on top of the cavitation plate with stainless steel bolts. Provided the leg is normally tilted out of the water, mild steel can be used. Steel tube or angle bar will be stiffer than aluminum. Galvanic action to the detriment of the aluminum parts of the outboard is possible with steel items attached to the leg, if the leg is left immersed in water. It is important to make the rudder blade extend down level with the lower tips of the propeller, otherwise a strong steering bias to one side or the other will result.

Troubleshooting at Sea

Outboards are popular for small weekend power cruisers which in calm conditions can hop from port to port at 20 knots (37 km/hr) or so. The boats are usually around 16 to 25 feet long, lightweight, with very shallow draft and hard-chine hulls. The same type of boat is often seen powered by a small outboard at nonplaning speeds. A better proposition if high speeds are not required is the round-bilge displacement hull, ballasted for extra stability. Open fishing launches come into this category, and they are a common sight at sea. Powered by outboards of 4 to 25 hp, they range from about 12 to 20 feet. These different craft constitute the types to be discussed below.

The main subject of this chapter is seaworthiness in relation to outboard-powered boats, and by this I mean the fitness of such boats to go to sea. Anyone can buy a boat, put an outboard on the transom, and head out to blue water. However seaworthy the hull, the boat as a whole may lack the equipment to carry its crew through any likely calamity. The most obvious thing that can happen is that the motor stops and will not start again. Relying on other people (even if possible) is unseamanlike: a boat should have the means to get itself out of difficulty, and this boils down to auxiliary power.

The consequences of the failure of a single motor must be faced and a plan of action conceived *before* going to sea. One only has to scan a few of the laconic accounts of Coast Guard rescues to be convinced. Coast Guard casualty statistics show that many incidents and deaths are connected with outboard-powered boats, particularly open ones, and frequently happen at night, which tends to suggest that they involve amateur fishermen.

Outboards give convenient and inexpensive propulsion, so

it is not surprising that most small craft from open rowing boats to mini-cruisers are so powered. As smaller boats are more numerous, and more likely to get into trouble anyway, it is not surprising that outboard motors are connected with so many incidents.

There are a few reasons why an outboard powered boat is less seaworthy. It is generally true that an outboard engine is slightly less reliable than an inboard: the constraints on its design (lightness, for instance) and its exposed position on the stern of a boat (accentuating deterioration when idle) see to that. And because it is exposed it is naturally more liable to cut out when heavy spray is flying around. It has to be said, though, that the modern motor is fairly resistant to this sort of treatment, as witness the 21-foot British Atlantic class lifeboats powered by twin 50-hp Evinrudes, and also the smaller inshore inflatable lifeboats.

An inboard engine constitutes a heavy weight placed low down, whereas an outboard is usually above the center of gravity of the boat, reducing its stability. In non-planing boats this can be compensated for by the addition of ballast (well-secured

Heading offshore in dirty weather is fine for fishermen, but there should be another power source on board in case the primary engine fails.

iron amounting to 10 to 20 percent of the boat's weight). As the propeller is farther away from the center of pitch and beyond the influence of the hull it is more affected by pitching and more likely to suck air. Swamping and pitching become more likely as the boat size increases and are two of the several reasons why outboard propulsion is less popular for seagoing motor boats of over 20 feet. Fuel costs are another factor.

Fast motor cruisers can hope to avoid being caught out in deteriorating weather. Their speed means that shelter can be reached in a shorter space of time—providing the motor keeps running and nothing else causes trouble.

Breakdown

Outboards (or any mechanical gadget, for that matter) do stop functioning from time to time, and it is the consequences of such a failure that can be so dangerous at sea. The greatest friend available is an anchor and rope; drift on to a lee shore is stopped, the boat wil ride more easily, and immediately there is less urgency in the situation. (A sea anchor, bulky and awkward though it may be, cuts drift in deeper water.) Cool, logical thought is required if engine trouble is to be diagnosed. Since the motor was running perfectly well only a few minutes before, it is mechanically all there and many possible faults can be eliminated right away. It is extremely rare for a piston rod to break or something as major to happen. Failure is usually a question of lack of fuel reaching the cylinder(s) or lack of spark. The very first (and easiest) things to check are that there is fuel in the tank and that the propeller is free from ropes or weed. A checklist such as the following, written on a card and carried on board, can be a blessing. Tools are needed, and some spare parts. The trouble might be simply a fouled plug, but without the means to remove it, and a replacement, you are absolutely stymied.

If it stops or won't start

Remember—to fire, a cylinder needs fuel in the right amount and a spark.

Phase 1   Check propeller for obstruction.
Check that fuel tap is on; with a gravity-feed integral tank, check that air vent is open.
Check fuel in tank.

Check that fuel is pumped up, using squeeze pump.
Try to restart.

If the motor starts and stops again, the fault is probably fuel starvation and could be caused by the engine fuel pump or a hose leak. The get-you-home solution is to keep squeezing the hand pump or hold the tank above the motor.

Phase 2   Take out spark plug (s).
Inspect and fit new one (s) correctly gapped (see handbook for correct gap).
Try to restart.

If the old plug is found to be wet there is too much fuel in the cylinder so, leaving the plug out, spin the engine over a few times with the throttle wide open and choke open (i.e. maximum air and minimum fuel) to dry out the cylinder.

Phase 3   (Getting down to business)
Check spark (as below).
Check fuel in float chamber (as below).
Try to restart.

Spark   Take out a plug and lay it on the cylinder with its HT lead attached. Spin the engine over: there should be a spark at the plug. Shade the plug with your hand in sunlight, but be careful not to touch it, especially with CD ignition, which gives an unpleasant electric shock. There may be sufficient energy to give a spark in the atmosphere but not under pressure in the cylinder, so if the spark seems weak hold the HT lead by its insulation $\frac{1}{4}$-inch away from the cylinder and spin the engine (not too fast). A spark should jump this gap easily. If the end of the HT lead is encased in a rubber boot, insert the end of an insulated screwdriver into the boot and hold it so that the screwdriver shank is $\frac{1}{4}$-inch away from some metal part of the engine. Another and rather easier way to check on the gap and jumping strength of the spark is to progressively bend out the side electrode of the plug to widen the gap. When playing around like this on an engine with CD ignition, beware of severe electric shock: it is not wise to hold the HT lead even by its insulation —use insulated pliers.

Fuel   Open the cock (if any) in the bottom of the float chamber and see if there is fuel there, or take off the top of the float chamber and look inside. Pull off the pipe connection to the carburetor and squeeze the hand pump to check that fuel is getting through. If there is no fuel in or reaching the carburetor, go back along the feed line to find the fault, which may be air leaks, pump failure or blockage. Ultimately one can lead the feed pipe from the tank direct to the carburetor and pump up fuel continuously by hand.

Phase 4   (Becoming difficult: probably impossible on the water)

Check jet for blockage and filters for dirt.

Check contact breakers (if fitted).

Try to restart.

Dismantle the carburetor and blow through the jet. From the handbook, find where the fuel filters are fitted and check them for dirt and water. If there is no spark or only a weak one, trace the HT leads and check for chafing or loose connections. You cannot do anything else with electronic ignition, and can only clean and correctly gap contact breakers of conventional systems. This entails taking off the rope starter housing and working through the window in the flywheel (if there is a window). A thin, fine file and feeler gauges are necessary; the handbook gives the correct gap. Afterwards clean the points, perhaps by inserting a clean handkerchief between them and pulling it out. Cleanliness is vital. If there is still no spark, you can only conclude that the coil has gone or maybe the timing has slipped.

After going through this procedure, you should be confident about the condition of the spark and whether fuel is getting into the cylinder in the right quantity. In other words the motor *should* start. But two-strokes are temperamental, and need coaxing on occasion. Try various combinations of throttle and choke, taking out a plug every ten starter pulls or so to check on wetness and spark. Another trick is to turn your back on the wretched thing and have a quiet smoke for ten minutes. In that time the excess fuel will have evaporated, the motor will have cooled off (and so will you), and it may occur to you what is wrong. Old HT coils sometimes age and give less voltage when warm.

A multi-cylinder engine with a single carburetor and single ignition system has no special diagnostic features, except that if one cylinder does not fire the fault is most likely to be the plug or its lead. Non-starting is less likely to be plug trouble. In a multi-cylinder engine with a separate carburetor for each cylinder and a single ignition system, non-starting is unlikely to be due to the carburetors, so concentrate on the common fuel line to the carburetors, and the spark. In multi-cylinder engines with a single carburetor and a separate ignition system for each cylinder, non-starting is not likely to be caused by HT genera-

Today, many small boats can take rough water. That and the twin out-boards let these anglers worry about the fish, not about getting home.

tion or plug faults, so concentrate on the carburetor and its fuel supply. Multi-cylinder engines with separate ignition and carburetor for each cylinder mean that one is virtually dealing with a number of self-contained engines. A fault in *all* carburetors or *all* ignition systems at once is unlikely, so concentrate on the common fuel supply.

The obvious tools to carry on board are large and small screwdrivers, pliers, a plug socket wrench, assorted double-ended wrenches and an adjustable, a file for the contact breakers, and feeler gauges for these and the plugs. Bits and pieces such as plastic tubing, electric cable, insulation tape, wire, nails and screws can be useful. Spares should include new sparkplugs, shear pins, a rope for the emergency starting pulley, and most important, the engine handbook.

Working over the transom while the boat is pitching and tossing is never easy, and there is the risk of tools or parts falling overboard. Ideally the motor should be brought inboard, but this again is not so easy. Taking the flywheel off to get at the contact breakers, or dismantling the leg to change the water pump impeller, are jobs which are nearly impossible at sea.

Emergency propulsion

Relying on just a set of tools and your diagnostic skill is not enough even within sight of land. Some other means of propelling the boat should be arranged. This can take many forms —another outboard, oars, paddles or a sail: it depends on the type of boat. An open boat of up to around 16 feet and having little windage can be successfully rowed if there are decent-length oars and proper oarlocks, or ideally, two sets of oarlocks and oars so that two people can combine their efforts. It's worth trying to row your boat for a distance before it happens to be necessary, just to learn whether the seats, foot room, oarlock heights, oar lengths, etc. make it practicable. Small changes in interior dimensions can make rowing far less tiring. Paddles are far less effective and not worthwhile. A short mast with a small simple sail such as a lugsail are possibilities on boats which have a relatively deep draft or a long keel to prevent too much leeway, and stowage space. Beating to windward may be impossible, but at least progress will be made downwind or across it. The hard-chine shallow draft cabin cruiser is suitable for neither rowing nor sailing, and the best answer is to carry a small get-you-home outboard. For this one wants an inexpensive, simple and robust motor with a good reduction ratio, but it need not have refinements such as silencing, gears or rubber mounts, and one obvious choice is the Seagull.

An emergency motor raises problems of stowage, and where to mount it on the transom, that are best worked out in advance. Does it require a different fuel mixture? Will it start when required? An upright stowage position in the cabin is ideal: it will then be protected against corrosion and be more liable to start when required. There may also be space under a berth or the foredeck. In any case, it should not be left to roll around, but secured firmly. When lifting it on to the transom, first secure it to the boat with a line. If it does need a different fuel mixture, a separate can must be carried, clearly marked with the mixture ratio, and old, stale fuel should not be left in its tank.

The ideal solution to the reliability problem is twin motors. A twin-motored boat even *looks* seamanlike, and the extra money spent over and above the cost of a single motor of equivalent power represents the greatest safety aid you could buy for your boat. (So does an emergency motor.) At the end of the earlier chapter on runabouts there are performance comparisons between twins and a single, and some of the advantages discussed will apply to other types of boats.

Another variation is the father-and-son idea: one large motor on the centerline is used for high speeds and a smaller offset motor for lower speeds. The small one can be left permanently in place alongside. Both motors then get their share of running, a defect of the emergency motor arrangement. Being on the transom at all times, the little motor is instantly ready to become the power to get you home (or get you out of danger if breakdown occurs at an awkward moment) without the possibly arduous task of shipping a stowed motor. If a good portion of the boat's running time is spent at non-planing speeds the small motor will pay its way in reduced fuel consumption.

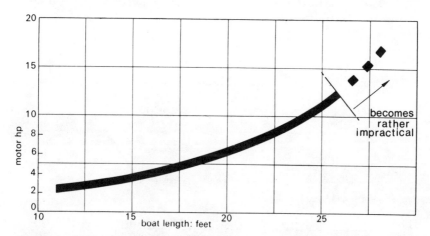

The graph shows emergency get-you-home outboard power for motor cruisers or small launches. Full-throttle running will be necessary for reasonable speed in calm water. There should be roughly 3 hp at least for every ton of boat weight. Over 25 feet a second small motor is probably a poor choice.

Engine breakdown must be considered well *before* you go to sea (whether inshore, offshore or in an estuary), and the best time to do this is when budgeting for the overall cost of the boat. Aim for the ideal of twin or father-and-son engines right from the outset, even if it means abandoning the idea of buying some luxury item.

Emergency power is also needed on single-engined inboard motor cruisers, and the outboard is often the simplest answer for small cruisers. In choosing a size of motor for this purpose a balance has to be struck between one which is too weak for the job and one which is powerful enough but too cumbersome to stow and too heavy to mount, besides being more costly. The windage of the boat is perhaps the most important factor determining whether a motor will be adequate. Against strong winds it may be difficult to keep steerage way or make progress; current plus wind is worse. The graph is intended to be a guide to the choice of power, but much depends on windage and the conditions in which propulsion will be needed. The problem is similar to that of powering a sailing yacht.

Reliability has a great deal to do with maintenance. In fact, I believe correct maintenance is a bigger factor in reliability than the choice of make of motor. But don't believe for one moment the sales brochure that implies that a particular make of motor will never let you down: 99.9 percent reliability is achievable—100 percent is not.

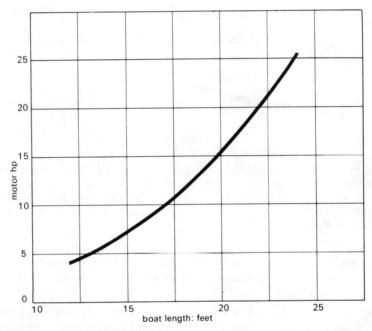

The graph shows sensible minimum motor size for estuary and seagoing non-planing motorboats. Much depends on the strength of local winds and tidal streams, and the boat's windage.

Minimum power

For non-planing boats there is a certain minimum power that is suitable for sea work, depending on the size of boat. The nature of the coast also has an influence. Tidal streams may run strongly, but in any case a strong wind and head sea can double or quadruple the horsepower necessary to maintain speed. A good margin over the calm water power adequate for canal or lake use is required, and below is a guide to this minimum power.

Range

An important aspect of using any boat on the sea is its range capability. Filling stations are few and far between on the coast, and there are no rescue patrols. A knowledge of the fuel consumption rate of your boat is essential. Very few outboard-powered boats can achieve more than 8 nautical miles to every gallon; more usually the figure is half as much. Even this lower figure can be halved again when heading against current or a wind and sea: the usual portable tanks for outboards are obviously not going to give much range. Apart from wanting to get to your destination (with plenty to spare to be on the safe side), it is most inconvenient to keep having to refuel, and one should aim at a calm water range of one or two hundred miles, knowing that it will be reduced sharply when conditions are less favorable. This implies a capacity of 25 to 50 gallons (95–190 L); this is a lot to carry for a small planing cruiser, so a compromise has to be struck.

One can see that large built-in tanks offer advantages over portable ones. To achieve a safe installation certain precautions have to be taken: any overflow must not be able to drain into the boat but must run overboard; tanks of over about 12 gallons (45 L) capacity should be vented with a pipe leading to the atmosphere outside the hull and terminating in a copper mesh flame arrester. The filler pipe should be more than 1½ inches (38 mm) in diameter, and bends should be avoided. Tanks can be made of most materials (except plain steel, which will rust inside) and should be mounted very securely, especially in planing boats, to brace them against pounding in a choppy sea. The fuel pipe to the motor should be of copper (*not* plastic) and terminate in the outboard well or outside the transom so that any leakage goes overboard. A filter at this point is a good idea. If the pipe terminates below the level of the top of the tank a fuel tap at the tank is necessary to avoid too much spillage when connecting and disconnecting, and also so that in the event of a fire the flow can be cut off. Filler caps in the deck or on the tank itself have to be absolutely watertight even if immersed.

Performance

The extra equipment and fuel needed for sea work add a considerable weight to the weekend power cruiser, so the minimum power for planing performance has to be increased accordingly.

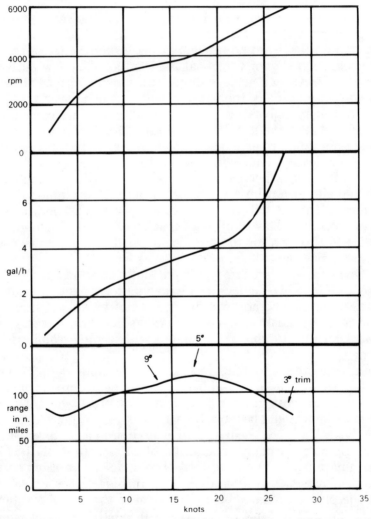

17-foot 6-inch (5.4 m) fiberglass cruiser (Shetland) in calm water. Trial weight 1900 pounds (870 kg) including two persons. Johnson 7-hp at 5000 rpm; 810 cc (49.7 cu. in.), three cylinders, three carbs, CD ignition, 2.4:1 reduction. The range curve is for calm water running with 24 gallons (91 L) of fuel.

This aspect, and the other points about tuning a fast boat, are similar to those discussed in the speedboat chapter. The important items here are the total range, the mpg (km/L) achieved, and the economical speed.

The performance of a 17-foot 6-inch fiberglass cruiser (Shetland 536) is shown above. Powered by a 70-hp Johnson, there is obviously plenty in reserve. The all-up weight on test was 1900 pounds (870 kg) including two crew, giving a power: weigth ratio of 3.7 hp/100 pounds (8.2 hp/100 kg). With 25 gallons (95 L) of fuel plus seagoing gear aboard, the weight would increase to around 2200 pounds (1000 kg) giving a ratio of 3.2 hp/100 pounds (7 hp/100 kg). The economical speed occurs at between 4000 and 4500 rpm and 16 to 20 knots (30 to 37 km/h) giving about 6 mpg (2.5 km/L). The range at various speeds is also given in (31), and an important point that emerges is that if a boat is forced off the plane by unbearable pounding its range suffers markedly—a worrying situation if this has not been taken into account when estimating the fuel required for the passage. Mpg curves (synonymous with range curves, being the distance travelled on a certain quantity of fuel) usually show a poorer situation off the plane, as can be seen in the curves for speedboats shown previously. Larger and heavier cruisers give the same shaped curves, but overall the mpg values are less: for a 20-foot planing cruiser one might be talking about only 2 mpg (0.8 km/L). Apart from the question of range, the weight and cost of all this fuel is considerable and it pays to run at the economical speed, i.e. where the boat is planing properly and comfortably (the nose has dropped after takeoff) but the throttle is by no means fully open.

Dinghies and Tenders

The ideal outboard motor for a yacht's tender should be light and self-contained, readily started when required, quiet running and non-drip when stowed in one's car. In practice this combination is rarely achieved, particularly as regards instant starting. All too often one sees some unfortunate owner tugging away at the rope start again and again, with no response. Of course in many cases it will be his fault, for over-choking, forgetting to switch on the fuel, and so on.

Before buying a little motor for your tender, reflect seriously on whether it's really warranted or not. To get out to the big boat, moored perhaps out in a lake or estuary, a motor may be more trouble than it's worth if the distance is short. The time and effort required to carry it from the car, fit it on to the dinghy, make sure it has fuel, and finally start it, may be greater than simply shipping a pair of oars and quietly rowing there. If the motor can safely be left on the dinghy, and if you do not have to launch from a beach or dock, matters are greatly simplified. A long distance out to the boat, or a strong current or a rather exposed mooring, are factors which put a different complexion on the decision. Another common justification for an outboard on a tender is in cruising, when there is often a fair distance to go to get ashore. Against a current or in strong winds a little outboard really pays its way, and encourages two trips to get everyone ashore safely, rather than overloading the boat to save time and effort and hoping all will be well. Even so, alternatives (cheaper ones, too) are used by many people— two sets of oarlocks and oars, or a simple sailing rig. In any case, to use the outboard automatically whenever you step into the dinghy is a bad habit. Practice in rowing is invaluable, especially for newcomers to boating, and using the outboard can

Inflatables make fine tenders, and because they are driven easily through the water, a wide range of outboards—from 2 to 50 hp in some cases—can be used.

sometimes be anti-social. On a calm summer's evening, who wants to hear the buzz of a motor? Sound carries very far across still water—and it is on still water that it is so easy to row.

The choice

The smallest tenders (those 7 to 8 feet long) are amply powered by the smallest motors available. Perhaps the most popular are the Johnson and Evinrude 2 hp, the Yamaha 2 hp and the Seagull 2 hp. This Seagull, like all the models in the range, is rather noisy and burns a smoky, oil-rich mixture, and does not have a recoil starter (although one is available from another firm). On the other hand, its popularity is assured by the low price, reliability and ruggedness. The other motors mentioned are quite quiet and smooth running, use lean mixtures, and have recoil starters. The weights of all four are similar at 20 to 24 pounds (9 to 11 kg), and they all have integral tanks. Other small motors include the Aquabug and the Neptune.

These small motors will adequately power much larger dinghies and inflatables, but if that extra half a knot and foaming wash is *really* required, then a larger motor is called for. Over-

97

powering is an all too common fault. The other big makes then come into the range of possibilities: the Volvo, Crescent and Archimedes 4 hp (all similar motors), the Mercury 4 hp, and the Chrysler 3.6 hp. All these motors are of rather similar mechanical specification, but some have separate rather than integral fuel tanks, or reverse gears rather than a 360° pivot reverse. Most are single cylinder; an exception is the Johnson/Evinrude 4 hp which has two cylinders with a separate ignition system for each, so that the chance of both cylinders ceasing to work is less likely. As always with low speed propulsion, a large reduction ratio and large propeller are an advantage. Apart from the Seagulls, the Volvo and Archimedes 5 hp have a good reduction ratio of 3 : 1.

A separate fuel tank makes any motor rather more bothersome to fit on to a dinghy, and takes up space. Gears can be considered as unnecessary sophistication and expense for dinghy work, but on the other hand, with direct drive the boat leaps forward as soon as the motor starts, which can be embarrassing or even dangerous, especially when the engine is cold and full throttle has to be applied. Some small motors are fitted with a clutch, which obviates this. A recoil started as opposed to a hand-wound rope is a great boon at all times, but especially when launching off a lee shore when seconds count, or in a strong current.

On the question of what size to choose, there are dangers in overpowering. A sudden start or stop or a swerve can tip the gunwale under. If the boat is overloaded, as is so often the case with yacht tenders, it may capsize. Two-hp motors are ample for the ubiquitous 7- to 8-foot minimum tender, hard or inflatable, and it is not until the 10 foot mark is reached before 4-5 hp should begin to be considered. In fact 10- to 12-foot dinghies that row easily are propelled quite adquately with 2-hp motors. Boats with wide and deeply immersed transoms do not come into this category—they drag water behind them and are also heavy to row. Dory-type dinghies and inflatables will plane given sufficient power, and this means motors of at least 10 hp on boats 10 to 14 feet long. They become miniature speedboats, and the comments in the appropriate chapter apply.

Precautions

It is wise to always tie the motor to the dinghy so that if it does fall or work its way off the transom at least it won't be lost. A simple way to do this is to arrange a short lanyard with a snap hook at the end, and a stout eyebolt on the transom. Many insurance companies take a dim view of paying for outboards lost overboard.

The tail-heavy dinghy with its single occupant necessarily sitting aft to steer the motor is a too-familiar sight. It is uncomfortable, and the speed potential is reduced. Two alternatives are an extended tiller so that one can sit on the center thwart and still steer, and perhaps still use the twist-grip throttle; or steering lines rigged forward to the center thwart. They can be simply tied on either side of the motor and lead through small blocks at the corners of the transom, and in a wide boat through similar pulleys on the center thwart.

On the big boat, a neat and convenient temporary stowage while under way can be arranged by sandwiching the stern pulpit with two vertical planks of thick plywood and clamping the motor to these, after clipping on the safety line. If the motor is to stay aboard more permanently, a sheltered position should be found. However weatherproof the motor may be, it will give a more troublefree and longer life if kept inside or in a locker. To prevent it rolling around and chipping off its protective finish, there should be a bar to which the motor can be clamped, preferably with the head above the leg. As with most bits of machinery, outboards have to be cosseted to give of their best. When the boat is laid up the motor is best taken home and after a little preventive maintenance stored in the garage or indoors.

Performance

Speed and fuel consumption have little relevance to outboards for tenders. All non-planing dinghies of the 7- to 12-foot size are taken up to close to their maximum displacement speed by the smallest motors (2 hp). While a 4-hp motor on a 10-foot dinghy will give the impression of giving much more speed, by virtue of the wash and noise created, this is very much an illusion: doubling the power may only in fact give another $\frac{1}{3}$ knot (0.6 km/hr). The punch needed to push a loaded boat into a chop and a strong wind or a foul tide is a better reason for choosing a bigger motor. A large reduction ratio in the gear hub is a sign that a motor will be superior in this respect (2:1 is average and 4:1 very good).

Static thrust is sometimes talked about as an indication of a small motor's punch. An average figure is about 20 to 25 pounds per hp (9–11 kg per hp). Tests tend to show that some of the high reduction ratio, big propeller outboards (such as Seagull and Whitehead) are classed in a horsepower rating such that they will propel a boat equivalently to other makes of conventional outboards. In other words, they will give equal thrust. This means that their actual horsepower produced, and consequently their fuel consumption, is a little less than for conventional but equivalent outboards. The bigger reduction ratio gives less fuel consumption rather than more thrust.

Usually there is a choice of only one or two propellers with these small motors, and again the only criterion is that at full throttle the motor should rev up to his full rated rpm.

Fuel consumption in this size range is around 1.2 pints (0.6 L) per horsepower per hour at full throttle, e.g. 2.4 pints an hour for a 2-hp motor. Normally range is not very important, but if it is, then work out whether an integral tank (which naturally tends to be rather small) will be sufficient or whether a remote tank will be required. If you like to take the dinghy off fishing or exploring, or it's a long way to your moorings across exposed water, consumption may be greater than the capacity of the integral tank.

What Every Owner Should Know

The fuel consumption of particular boat/engine combinations has been mentioned in preceding chapters, and at this point it is worth having a general round-up of this topic. The more power an engine produces the greater is its fuel consumption; the amount of power produced from the fuel consumed is a measure of the engine's efficiency. Diesel, gasoline, steam or electric engines give different efficiencies dependent on design limitations. The two-stroke engines in outboard motors generally give the following consumptions per horsepower:

	pints/hp/hour	*L/hp/hour*
up to 10 hp	1.1–1.3	0.52–0.63
10–40 hp	1.0–1.2	0.46–0.57
above 40 hp	0.8–1.0	0.4–0.46

Notice that fuel economy and therefore the efficiency improves as the motor size increases, due to the increased size of the combustion chamber. These figures apply at full throttle, so they are only useful in working out the approximate maximum consumption of a particular motor. In practice outboards do not (or should not) run at full throttle for very long, and for average use the likely consumption over a period of many running hours will be about half of the maximum. This would not be true for canal cruising or fishing where the necessarily low revs will mean an even lower average fuel consumption. In terms of distance travelled on a given quantity of fuel (i.e. mpg), outboard-powered boats generally achieve no more than about 6.5 miles per gallon (3.2 km/L) at the very best, whatever the boat or engine. The fuel mileage achieved in most cases is more likely to be 4 mpg (2 km/L) or less.

At any speed very much less than full throttle, the two-stroke engine burns fuel less efficiently than it does at full throttle, so the figures for volume/hp/hour increase as the throttle is reduced. This is not nearly as typical of four-stroke gasoline engines or diesel. Consequently, when comparing the fuel consumption of various engines in boats at *cruising* speeds, the outboard motor comes out even worse than is shown by the full-throttle comparison. Occasionally one sees specific fuel consumption curves, for inboard engines, and they show flatter

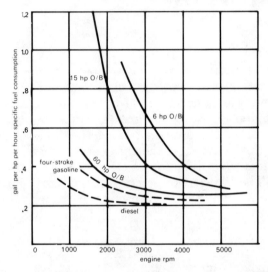

The increasing inefficiency of two-stroke outboards as the throttle is reduced. Bigger capacity motors are shown to be more efficient than small motors. The tests were run on modern outboards powering typical boats.

curves than indicated in the graph because they relate to an engine running on a test bed at full throttle, the rpm being varied by varying the load. In a boat, the rpm is varied by the throttle setting, and only at high revs is full throttle applicable; it is for the boat condition that the above curves are drawn.

The conversion of fuel energy into horsepower at the crankshaft by combustion is only one half of the story: the other half is the conversion of this output power into propeller thrust. The two-stroke outboard is inefficient in converting fuel to power because of the limitations of the two-stroke cycle. Unfortunately, it also suffers in transmission when used at low boat speeds because of the small, inefficient propellers usually fitted. The overall result shows up in the tests mentioned in the chapter on inland use, comparing a 6-hp diesel with a 6-hp outboard on similar boats; the respective mpgs were 34 and 10, or 11 and 3 km/L.

Overall efficiency

It is interesting to pursue this theme a little further. A gallon of fuel contains a certain amount of energy; if gasoline is burned at the rate of a gallon (3.8 L) every hour, the energy released is equivalent to 44 horsepower. In other words, if an engine were 100 percent efficient it would produce 44 hp when consuming 1 gal/hr. Taking our previous figures of specific fuel consumption—let's use 1.0 pints/hp/hr (0.47 L)—an outboard will only give 6.6 hp when consuming a gallon (8 pints) an hour. The other 37.4 hp has been lost somewhere, and the engine efficiency is only 6.6 divided by 44 = 15 percent. This is achieved at *full* throttle; at lower throttle settings the engine efficiency is still lower. We can see the combined effect of the engine's inefficiency at cruising, and the transmission and propeller inefficiency, by comparing the fuel input with the towrope horsepower,—our test on a 17-foot 6-inch cruiser with a modern motor. At 4 knots (7.4 km/hr) the towrope pull was 46 pounds

This particular bass boat is running at nearly full throttle, the point at which two-stroke engines are the most fuel-efficient.

(21 kg), giving a towrope horsepower of 0.5. This is the end result of the fuel conversion process, while the input was 3.6 pints (1.7 L) per hour which on the fuel energy basis works out as the equivalent of 20 hp. So in fact only $\frac{1}{2}$ hp out of a potential 20 was actually being used to push the boat along—an overall propulsion efficiency of $2\frac{1}{2}$ percent. By contrast, a diesel in the same boat at the same speed would give a slightly more attractive figure of around 10 percent.

This discussion is not meant to persuade you to go diesel, but presented for academic interest. The four-stroke gasoline engine would give efficiency and fuel consumption figures somewhere in between the two-stroke and the diesel, which is a strong argument for a four-stroke outboard for boats travelling at displacement (i.e. non-planing) speeds.

Outboard motors are much more efficient when operating as designed on speedboats. For instance in the dory test mentioned in the chapter on runabouts, when the correct propeller was fitted to the 60-hp motor the thrust given by the motor at full throttle was about 560 pounds (255 kg). The boat was running at 27 knots (50 km/hr) giving a towrope horsepower of 45. The fuel consumption was 6.3 gallons an hour (24 L/hr), equivalent to a fuel horsepower of 280. Thus the overall efficiency was 16 percent, a relatively good figure achieved in part because here the propeller was able to work at a high efficiency (about 70 percent). The gear ratios and consequent propeller sizes of most outboards are designed for higher boat speeds: thus, in a speedboat the transmission efficiency is high, and because the motor is running at a high throttle opening, the engine is reasonably efficient. Moreover, the motor's light weight adds to the overall performance of the boat. It is at displacement speeds on slow motor cruisers and sailing boats that the efficiency of both propeller and engine drop to dismal proportions.

On a planing boat the best fuel mileage is achieved when it is planing properly but by no means at full throttle. On a displacement boat it is achieved when the boat slips easily through the water without fuss or excessive wash nor in a bows-up attitude. In terms of gallons per hour, the slower you go the less the consumption whatever the type of boat or engine.

More on propellers

The correct choice of propeller is essential. Propellers are sized by their diameter and pitch, in that order. The correct size is

If pressure on the back faces of the blades drops enough to allow the water flowing past them to vaporize, this is called cavitation. The suction faces are then working in a kind of air pocket. Most props are designed to cavitate slightly, but the above cavitation is excessive. The prop will race, straining the engine, and water slamming back on the blades will erode the metal.

simply the one that allows the motor at full throttle to rev up to an rpm within the manufacturer's recommended band. On slower cruisers the bottom end of the band is ideal; on most other boats the middle is ideal. The same motor on different hulls having different speed potentials will require different propellers. The greater the top speed the larger the pitch required.

A right-handed propeller is one which rotates clockwise when in ahead, when viewed from astern; a left-handed propeller rotates counterclockwise. The handing cannot be changed: turning the propeller around does not change it.

It is possible to bend the blades of a propeller to change the pitch, but this can only be done for small changes of an inch or so, and all the blades must be bent identically. This is virtually impossible to do accurately without a special pitch measuring device, and the consequences of a badly set propeller are vibration and wear on the bearings, so it is a job best left to the manufacturer or repairer. When a propeller becomes badly chipped or bent it can usually be repaired more cheaply than buying a new one, and various firms specialize in repair and rebuilding, or will exchange propellers.

To achieve thrust in a liquid medium a propeller must slip to some extent, in other words it will not advance a distance equal to its pitch for every revolution. The greater the slip the less the efficiency of the propeller. The bigger the propeller for a given horsepower the slower it has to turn to absorb that power, and the less slip involved. A large, slow-turning propeller requires a larger reduction gear ratio between engine and propeller.

Cavitation causes excessive slip and so too does aeration—the sucking of air down from the surface into the propeller. The two are often confused. Occasionally, sudden and excessive slip and consequent engine racing may be caused by slippage of the rubber hub in the propeller boss, and it is easy to blame this on cavitation. An outboard dealer can torque-test the rubber hub, which is there to protect the gears against the shock of propeller impact (not, as is sometimes assumed, to protect the propeller itself, although it does that to some extent).

Electrolysis

Aluminum, which most outboard legs are made of, is low down in the electrochemical series, which means that it is attacked by most of the other common metals used in boats. Any fittings made of brass, copper, bronze, mild steel or cast iron will attack the surface of an aluminum leg if both are immersed in seawater and are electrically connected, i.e. if there is a conducting path (other than the water) for current to flow between them. Fiberglass boats are unlikely to have a large amount of one of these metals close to the motor, let alone electrically linked, so electrolysis from this direction is rarely a problem. If a bronze propeller is fitted, electrolytic corrosion is quite likely, and one or two of the major manufacturers offer cathodic protection units to neutralize the effect. A simpler and cheaper way out is *always* to tilt the motor out of the water when it is not in use: this is a good idea whether a bronze propeller is fitted or not. Stainless steel (propellers, bolts, etc.) is compatible with aluminum. The other probable cause of electrolytic action is via copper-based antifouling; if the leg is left in the water corrosion is certainly likely to take place. Either tilt the leg, or use a non-copper antifouling suitable for aluminum hulls.

Theft

This aspect of owning an outboard motor seems to grow steadily in importance. From a thief's point of view, an outboard

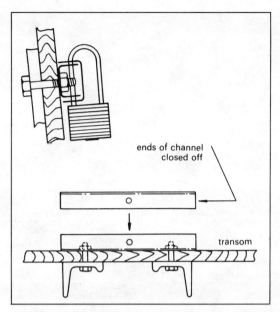

ends of channel
closed off

transom

Locking the nuts of the motor bracket bolts.

represents a valuable and readily disposable article that is often easily acquired. Insurance companies will not normally cover an outboard unless it is attached to the boat by an approved locking arrangement, which often means approval by their surveyor. Manufacturers appear to pay little heed to the problem other than supplying, as an accessory, a lock to go over the clamp screws. The time has come for standard motors to have a convenient, designed-in key locking device which will satisfy the insurers.

There are perhaps two different types of theft to guard against, the first being casual in the sense that a small motor left on a tender is stolen while its users are away. The other types involves the more determined thief armed with bolt-cutters and hacksaws, looking for a bigger motor on a boat left ashore or swinging idly on her mooring during the week. For the first situation one merely wants a deterrent. Any number of simple precautions can be thought of, including the type of lock which consists of a tube with a long slot into which the clamp screws fit, the whole thing being locked with a padlock or built-in lock. Some of those on the market give little protection against a determined thief: a brass tube would be easy meat for a variety of tools. Corrosion resistant or marine padlocks are available from chandlers and locksmiths.

This engine is mounted in an outboard well. The well provides for proper mounting while preventing the wash and waves from entering over a low transom.

Small motors usually have transom brackets with two clamp screws, medium power motors usually have two clamps and two bolt holes for bolting through the transom, while the larger motors dispense with screw clamps and rely on four or more bolts. Where bolts are used they act as a deterrent, and if the nuts can be "locked" security is even higher; some nuts require a special tool to remove them (as on expensive car wheels). A steel channel-section padlocked in place can be used to cover the nuts. If an oversize bolt can be fitted there may be room to drill a hole through its nut corresponding to a hole in the bolt so that a padlock hasp can be passed through both. Where the motor cannot be bolted in place, a hefty J-bolt through the transom with the J hooking on to some part of the motor bracket can be devised, the nut being locked by one of the means already described. On Seagull motors in particular the securing pin which slides athwartships through the bracket can be made to give some protection: a hole is drilled in the

The British Seagull is a simple outboard with most components accessible for repair. The five-bladed prop provides great power at low speeds.

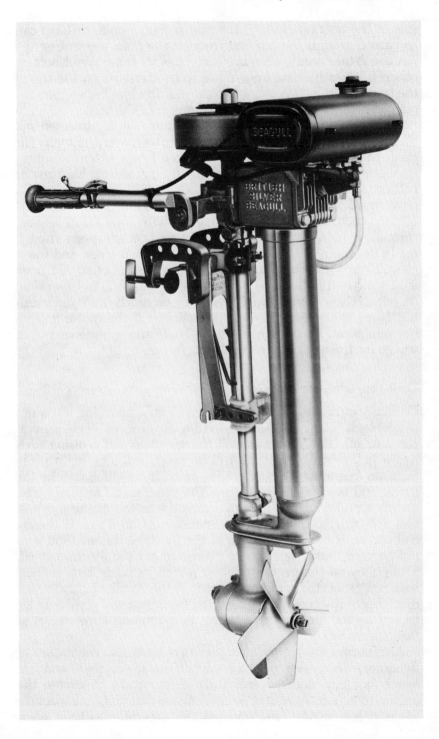

side of the bracket close to the pin so that a padlock hasp can be passed around the pin and through the hole, preventing the pin being taken out. This is sufficient with the Seagull bolt-on bracket, but otherwise an eye has to be arranged on the top of the transom in between the two sides of the bracket so that the pin can pass through it, locking the motor to the boat.

Many varieties of locking arrangement can be dreamed up. The degree of protection depends a great deal on the materials used. Mild steel, brass, bronze and to a lesser extent stainless steel are relatively soft materials easily cut with a hacksaw or bolt-croppers. Hardened steel is better, although one would have to go to really exotic alloys to get total protection. One obvious method is to have a chain or wire rope strop passing through a hole in the transom and padlocked—even though really determined thieves have sawed through wood and fiberglass. Even with tough materials there is the snag that the strop is inevitably a little loose and can be pulled out, to be worked on relatively easily. Locked nuts may be much more inaccessible. None of these means will be sufficient if the motor and its fastenings can be wrenched off the boat: the experienced thief will go for the weakest link in the chain.

Do-it-yourself generators

On many outboard motors where an electric charging kit is not available, it is not too difficult to fit a car or motorcycle generator yourself. The generator will charge at normal cruising revs, and a hefty current output will be produced. The main problems are in finding a place on the engine from which to take the drive, and somewhere to mount the generator. On many outboards a pulley can be mounted directly on top of the flywheel and a belt drive taken to the generator, as on a car. If the recoil starter is mounted on top of the flywheel this method cannot be used, but a belt can be taken around the flywheel itself. The pulley on the generator should then be fairly large, otherwise the generator could overspeed: if the flywheel is twice the diameter of the generator pulley the generator will revolve twice as fast as the motor; three times the diameter, three times as fast, and so on.

Alternators are happy at higher revs than DC generators or dynamos. They also produce current at lower revs, and are less bulky but more expensive. It is important to choose the engine-to-generator revs ratio carefully so that charging will take place at low engine revs, and yet the generator will not overspeed at full throttle. For slow cruising, fishing, canals and river boating a step-up in speed may be required, say a 3-inch (75 mm) diameter pulley on the generator and one of 5-inch (125 mm) on the engine. Pulleys and belts intended for small motors, lawnmowers, lathes, etc. can be adapted to outboards.

Motorcyle alternators are very compact and may fit inside the outboard cover or hood, but it is not very difficult to add a fiberglass power bulge to the hood itself. One alternator that has been used in a conversion (on a 20-hp Chrysler outboard) is a 12 V Lucas model that is normally fitted to Triumph 650 motorcycles: it gives 6 to 8 A. Another obvious (and low-cost) generator that could be used (and has been used on a Johnson 6) is a car type, but because of its bulk it will probably have to be mounted outside the hood with a big slot for the belt. The question of waterproofing then comes up, unless a whole new and enlarged hood is made.

Naturally a generator absorbs power from the motor, and the smaller the motor the more noticeable this becomes (a 12 V generator giving 30 A will absorb up to about 1 hp). The control box or regulator can be standard car or motorcycle equipment mounted inboard in the dry. An ammeter in the circuit is useful to prove the system and show how many amps are being produced. A 30 or 40 amp hour (AH) battery is adequate for most small cruisers. To calculate the required capacity, one can add up roughly how many amps for how many hours will be required between engine runs, using lighting and appliance ratings, and allowing for the heavier drain of starting current (1 amp hour = 1 amp for one hour); voltage depends on the generator output.

Any modification such as fitting a generator or adapting the motor to run on kerosene naturally invalidates any maker's or seller's warranty.

Noise

It is not very often that one sees attempts by boatbuilders or owners to carry on the silencing built into most modern outboards. Modern motors with rubber mounts, hoods and underwater exhausts are reasonably quiet, but sometimes the inner surface of the hood is not lined with noise absorber. Either ½-inch (13 mm) or 1-inch (25 mm) thick polyurethane foam will help a little, or if weight is no problem a foam/lead/foam sandwich sheet is better. Another way to reduce noise is to box in the motor completely, or cover it with a noise hood rather like

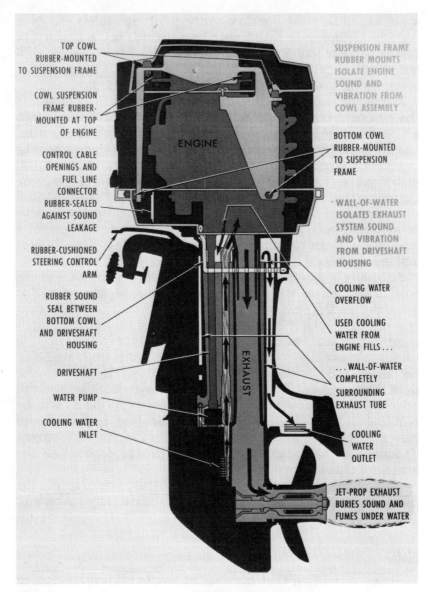

The modern outboard engine, though by no means silent, contains numerous sophisticated techniques for dampening and diffusing its sound.

those one sees over public telephones.

Complete boxing-in may cause the motor to be starved of air or choke on its own fumes, so ventilation is very necessary: unfortunately, where air can get in, sound can get out. The

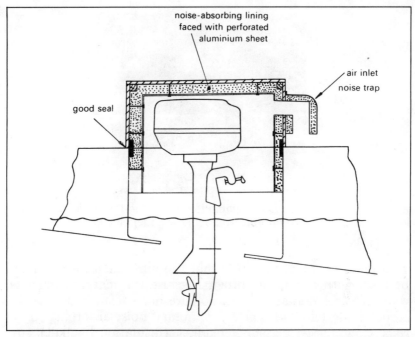

Boxing in an outboard which is fitted in a trunk, to reduce noise.

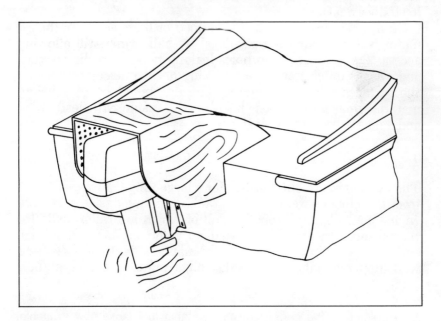

A noise hood. There should be a good seal where it joins the boat. The whole thing can be hinged at its forward edge for access.

113

An on board tachometer is essential for measuring the engine's perform-ance, finding the correct prop, and achieving fuel efficiency.

vital point about boxing-in is that the internal surfaces should be lined with a noise absorber. Because the material must be waterproof or non-absorbent, polyurethane foam is out, as are carpet underfelt and many proprietary noise-absorbing mate-rials. Compressed glassfiber blanket (insulation blanket) cov-ered with perforated aluminum is one answer, and glassfiber itself does not burn.

On many cruisers a detachable hood or lid over the outboard motor well can cut the noise level by half, while still allowing access. There must be no holes leaking noise into the cockpit, and a lid is much improved by lining it with noise-absorber on the surfaces facing the motor. The lid should be of a heavy material; marine plywood, lined on the inside with lead sheet and a noise absorber, is ideal.

Accessories

The big makers of outboards offer a large range of extras. Apart from the obvious items such as tanks, steering systems, remote engine controls and propellers, all of which are tailor-made for the motors concerned and need no comment here, there are such things as instruments, maintenance aids, handbooks and workshop manuals, fixed tanks, bilge pumps, storage stands,

At left, some of the permanent and portable fuel tanks now available. Gas is highly volatile—containers must be of high quality and properly installed.

canvas covers, and also items mentioned above such as brackets and electrical kits.

Most outboard fuel tanks are made of steel, which have a problem in that after a time they leave rusty marks where they lie. Some manufacturers use plastic for their tanks; however, in the event of fire the plastic will melt fairly readily, with disastrous consequences.

A tachometer (rev counter) is a very necessary instrument for fast boats. Water temperature (or water pressure) gauges give warning of cooling failure which could lead to expensive engine seizure. The cooling water outlet is usually arranged to be clearly visible on outboards in order that water circulation can be checked, but the stream of water may not be visible from the helm, or may be forgotten about after a period of trouble-free running. An ammeter is really essential if you have electric charging or starting. Maintenance aids include lubricants, cleaners, paint, storage oils, and flushing attachments for use with a garden hose.

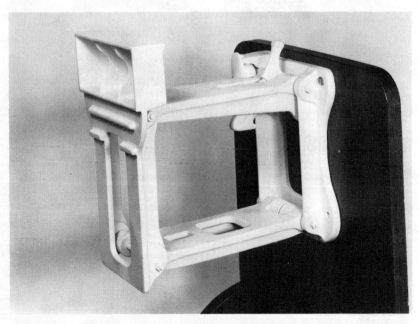

There is great variety in the kinds of outboard engine brackets now on the market. The handiest allow adjustments in height of the power head off the water, and facilitate lifting the outboard clear.

Outboard boats are almost always trailable. The important thing here is the security of the boat and engine—tie the boat down amidships and at the bow, and mark the extreme after projection of the outboard leg with a bright red flag.

Trailering

A point to note about trailering a boat with an outboard on it is that in some countries (including the UK) a motor leg protruding beyond the stern—especially if tilted up—is considered a dangerous load in the eyes of the law. Common sense also suggests that a pedestrian, cyclist or motorcyclist would be seriously injured by the motor if he was hit by it or ran into it. So the sensible thing to do if the motor cannot be taken off is to wrap the leg in heavy sacking or anything that will similarly reduce the danger, and also hang an easily-seen flag on the extreme end.

How to Keep Your
Motor Running

To get the best from a motor, particularly in terms of reliability, requires some conscious thought on the owner's part, when running it and when it is idle. An outboard also requires regular attention to parts which gradually wear out or get blocked up, sparkplugs and filters being two obvious items. Just as for cars, there is a list of jobs to be performed at specific intervals of running time or months; most of them are quite simple and do not require special tools. It is so much more sensible to do them at the specified times than leave them until the motor stutters to a halt in the middle of an otherwise enjoyable day (it may be more than inconvenient if you are without a second means of propulsion). Special tools are required as one starts to delve into the gearbox or the guts of the engine itself, but that is in the category of major repairs; there should normally be no need to take the engine or gearbox to pieces over most of the service life of a motor. In any case, because of the workshop skill and special tools required, most of the main manufacturers strongly discourage amateur interference in the depths of their motors. For some of the smaller, less sophisticated motors the position is rather different.

Rather than attempt to give detailed workshop manual instructions, which would be impossible in a small book, I will dwell on the more commonplace aspects of looking after outboards: how to fuel and run them, how to prevent damage on deterioration through happy ignorance, and how to do simple maintenance and simple repairs. Looking after the motor yourself of course saves money, but it also has the great merit that one becomes acquainted with its idiosyncrasies and familiar

Beaching an outboard boat in shallow water requires an awareness of bottom characteristics to avoid damaging the prop or sucking sand through the pump.

with the parts which are likely to fail out on the water: you are more likely to be able to diagnose trouble and deal with it on the spot—a part of basic seamanship.

Some do's and don'ts

Many outboard troubles stem from the fuel/oil mixture being of the wrong proportions or containing the wrong grade of gasoline or oil. Be absolutely sure of the correctness of the fuel, whether it is a two-stroke mixture or not.

Whenever the leg is immersed there is a chance that water will get into the gearcase via the propeller shaft seal, and this becomes more likely as the motor gets older and the seal becomes worn. Any water in there—particularly seawater—does the gears and bearings no good at all. Another reason for tilting the leg up is to avoid possible electrolytic corrosion and marine fouling (or alternatively, having to antifoul the leg). Propeller blade smoothness is important, particularly on fast boats, and naturally a propeller stays cleaner out of the water. One exception to the general rule of always tilting up the motor occurs when the air temperature drops below freezing: any water left in the water pump could freeze, expand and crack the housing, so in such conditions it is better to leave the leg in the water. On the other hand, if the temperature drops low enough and for long enough to freeze the water (or even the sea) it is better to keep the motor out and make sure the pump and water passages are empty by spinning the motor with the starter a few times (remove the sparkplug leads to prevent it starting).

Flush the cooling passages through with fresh water after running in salt or polluted water (this is a common makers' recommendation). Two ways of doing the job are to run the motor in a tank of fresh water, or to feed the intake grid or hole from a garden hose (adapters are available as accessories).

After running in salt or polluted water, the cooling system should be flushed. One method is to run the engine in a tank of freshwater. Another method is to force freshwater from a hose into the intake port.

This is easier said than done, particularly if the motor is normally left on the boat, and in fact it is so impractical that most people do not bother even if it is the tender's motor and normally taken home each time. The least one should do is to flush the system if the motor is to be idle for a long period—over the winter for instance, or if it is not going to be used for a month or two for some reason. Flushing washes away the salt and other chemical deposits inside the engine, which cause so much more corrosion to metal parts than clean fresh water. Still on corrosion prevention, try to preserve the external surface coating of the motor and avoid knocks and scratches. When it is going into the car, wrap it up in old rags. Don't leave it to scrape against the garage floor for the winter, or put it in a locker on the boat among other sharp metal gear. Most motors make use of aluminum for lightness; although in general fairly corrosion resistant, it suffers from crevice corrosion. Where there is even the tiniest crevice in which water can collect, a white jelly-like hydroxide forms; it can be seen wherever the bare metal has been in contact with fresh or, especially, salt water. It also means that bolts threaded into aluminum can seize up solid. Corrosion occurs far more rapidly in salt water, and continues after the motor has been lifted out of the water unless the salt is washed off completely. Salt is hygroscopic: it absorbs moisture, so on damp days surfaces which have even a little dried-on salt become quite wet and corrosively very active. Coatings applied in manufacture are meant to prevent water getting into contact with the aluminum, but the surface can be chipped away.

Never tilt the leg *above* the horizontal directly after the motor has been running, or even if the leg has been in the water. Any water remaining in the exhaust tube may well run back into the cylinder and subsequently cause rusting. Left for any length of time, it could wreck the engine. Only motors which are entirely air cooled (some have air cooled heads and water cooled exhausts) and where the exhaust is not ejected underwater are free from this caution. This point is one always to bear in mind when carrying an outboard or putting it into a car, or when arranging a clamping bracket for stowage in a locker: the motor should not be horizontal but slightly leg-down.

A handbook is usually supplied with the motor; if it is not, or if the motor is secondhand, be sure to get one (they are quite inexpensive). Whether you are technically minded or not, it is essential to know such things as the correct fuel/oil mix, the grades of gasoline and oil to use, the necessary gearcase oil, and the sparkplug and gap specifications. Don't rely on a knowledgeable friend, because working on approximations or wrong assumptions can lead to endless frustration, poor running and expense.

One might naturally think that putting a cover over the head when the motor is idle is a good idea, but this is not always so. For motors which have enclosed powerheads (usually the hood is fiberglass) it's rather unnecessary: the works are covered already, and there is the possibility of more condensation on the cold metal surfaces of the engine than would otherwise form. Condensation plays havoc with ignition systems. In no circumstances should a plastic bag be put over the motor, especially a transparent bag; there will be no chance of ventilation, and the motor will sweat on colder days and fry in its miniature greenhouse in sunshine. The cover is best made of a material which will breathe, in other words canvas, and even then the bottom edge should be left quite loose to allow air to circulate. On exposed engines like Seagulls such a canvas cover is undoubtedly a good thing.

Starting trouble is sometimes due to a too-oily mixture in the float chamber, or to the evaporation of the more volatile constituents of the fuel mixture. When the motor is idle the gasoline evaporates from the float chamber, and eventually the tank (especially on hot days), leaving a residue of oil. When fuel is pumped up in order to start the motor the first bowlful

Idling for a length of time will cause carbon to build up in the engine. If you need to remain stationary, shut the engine off and anchor.

Regularly check to see that water is exiting from your cooling system.
This water-cooled outboard is functioning perfectly.

of fuel to go into the cylinder has twice as much oil as it should
have. It used to be a well-known trick to drain the carburetor
after stopping the engine, or more simply to disconnect the pipe
from the tank and allow the motor to use up the fuel remaining
in the float chamber and run to a halt. With 50:1 mixtures and
high-voltage ignition this precaution is probably unnecessary,
but on the other hand there are some motors which still run on
30:1 or even more oily mixture ratios.

Running slowly for long periods causes carbon to build up
inside the cylinder and on the sparkplugs, so avoid idling for
very long, or continuous slow running. Some of the carbon can
be burned off by a short burst at high revs. If slow running is
normal usage, fit a hotter plug than recommended to at least
reduce plug fouling.

Treat the snap-on fuel pipe connections to the remote tank
gently. Heavy-handed pushing, or trying to put the connections
on the wrong way around, can damage the O-ring seals and
cause leaks. Since the tank is usually below the level of the
carburetor a leak will cause air to seep in rather than fuel to
seep out, with the result that the motor keeps stalling because
the fuel pump cannot keep the float chamber topped up.

Disconnect the fuel line at the tank when leaving the boat
for the week. This is just a precaution against the possibility
of a leak in a part of the pipe below the level of the fuel in the
tank, in which case it would slowly syphon out of the tank and
into the boat.

Most water cooled motors have a tell-tale stream of water
issuing from the leg or the underside of the head to show that

Continuous running at full throttle will shorten the life of an outboard engine, as will drag-boat starts and sudden stops from high speed.

the water pump is working. Failure of the pump leads to over-heating and eventual seizure: at full throttle this may occur within minutes and disastrously. So it is wise to glance at the tell-tale every now and then. In shallow water be careful not to allow the leg to hit bottom or stir up sand which may then be sucked into the water pump and cause excessive wear.

Never run a water cooled motor out of the water (at least not for more than a few seconds) otherwise the pump impeller will run dry and will probably be damaged. Only air cooled motors with neither water cooled exhaust nor water lubricated bearings can safely be run out of the water.

Many running problems occur because the wrong propeller is fitted. Only a tachometer can tell you if the propeller fitted is the correct one (see the discussion on propellers elsewhere in this book).

Do not force the gear lever into ahead or astern with the motor stopped. If the dogs happen *not* to be lined up with each other, they will never slip into engagement no matter how hard the gear lever is pushed: the gear push rods and other links will bend first. If the motor is stopped in gear the dogs will slide apart, so one can safely move the gear lever to neutral.

Move the gear shift lever *firmly* into ahead or astern. There is not a plate clutch (as on a car) which needs gentle engagement but a dog clutch which is either in or out, with no halfway stage.

Hesitant engagement merely burrs the teeth of the dogs and eventually they become harder to engage or keep slipping out.

Rapid wear of the dog clutches will occur if the idling speed of the motor is set higher than specified in the manual, or if the gear lever is pushed into gear when the motor is revving up. The idle adjustment (a throtle stop on the carburetor) should be set to the specified revs with a tachometer, ideally, or by reducing the idling speed of the warm engine to the lowest point at which it runs smoothly and reliably without stalling.

Running for long life

Like any other engine, an outboard motor lives longer if full throttle is only applied for short periods, with each burst followed by a longer period at three-quarter throttle. Similarly, it is better in the long run not to slam on full throttle with a cold engine, nor to suddenly shut down and stop from full throttle. Because the engine is small in size it does not take long to warm up, especially with a thermostat. A choke is usually fitted for cold starts, and used as on a car; push the choke in as soon as the motor will run without it. Before pulling the starter cord make sure the fuel is switched on or pumped up, and the throttle opened slightly and the gear lever in neutral. If the engine is warm it should start without choke; if there is some doubt, try to start without choke because the plugs may become wet with fuel if the engine is choked unnecessarily. To clear the engine of excess fuel, apply full throttle, push in the choke, and switch off or unplug the fuel supply—maximum air, minimum fuel—and spin the motor over several times. When pulling the cord, take up the slack first before pulling hard. On the return, allow the cord to wind in completely before releasing the handle.

On a small dinghy with just one person on board who is trying to start the outboard and necessarily sitting right aft, it is quite likely that the underwater exhaust outlet is more deeply immersed than normal, and this creates back pressure which may lead to starting trouble. There is not much that can be done if one is alone on board, but otherwise the crew can sit right in the bows. Starting trouble may also be due to an insufficient head of fuel because of the trim. If there is little fuel in the motor-mounted tank and also the motor is inclined backwards due to the trim of the boat, it is possible that fuel never gets to the carburetor. Alternatively this can lead to kangaroo stops and starts: as the boat gathers speed and the bows rise, the carburetor is starved of fuel; as it slows, fuel again reaches the carburetor and the motor picks up again.

All engines ultimately give better life if they are properly run-in from new. The object is to bed in the surfaces which rub together within the engine, and to rinse out metal swarf and debris with lubricant. The first hour is the most important time, and the engine should be run at low revs (up to 2000–3000 rpm). Afer that, full throttle should only be applied for very short bursts, for instance to get a planing boat up on the plane, in the next few hours. (Details of exactly what to do are always given in the handbook.) Sometimes an extra oily fuel mixture is recommended.

The opposite of gentle running-in is occasionally recommended: for example, the Seagull handbook says that the bearings are so large that under light load polishing of the internal surfaces will not happen, and consequently heavy usage is recommended right from the beginning.

For the very first run try to choose quiet conditions with plenty of time in hand so that you can get used to the motor and controls. Make allowances for its initial stiffness.

After a few hours' running the engine will have settled down. The cylinder head gasket will have compressed and consequently the cylinder head bolts will be under-tight. The gears will have shed particles of metal, and the contact breaker gap may have closed up as the cam follower has bedded in. Consequently most manufacturers recommend a service at around 10 hours' running time to tighten bolts, change the gear oil, and re-set the contact breakers among other things. Sometimes this service is done free by the dealer; it may be obligatory in order not to invalidate the warranty.

Tilting mechanisms

Practically all outboards can be tilted up to about 60° to the vertical. Apart from other benefits, this allows the leg to kick up if it hits an underwater obstruction: otherwise the transom might be wrenched off. In order that reverse does not tilt the motor up a locking lever is usually provided. It should normally be in the lock position, which may seem in contradiction to the purpose of the device, but the lock position, while stopping the

The locking device, which keeps the leg down when in reverse, will allow the leg to rise if the leg is struck with enough force.

motor tilting up when in reverse, does actually allow the leg to tilt if a really hard backwards force is applied at the bottom of the leg, as when hitting something. On most outboard boats the leg projects below the bottom or keel, and one has to bear this in mind when approaching a beach or shallow water. Considerable damage can be done to the leg and propeller if it churns into sand, stones or even mud.

The pivot which allows tilting usually has adjustable friction and this should be set so that the leg slowly drops down to the running position when the motor is released. Too free and the motor bangs down; too tight (or jammed) and the emergency kick-up will be affected. Similarly, the pivot which enables the motor to be steered often has an adjustable friction nut. Minimum friction is required for remote steering, but a small amount for hand steering.

Safety precautions

Whenever fuel is being handled, nobody in the vicinity should smoke: an obvious precaution, it is one that is so easy to forget. Another caution around the safety theme is to beware of rotating parts. A propeller thrashing around is a very dangerous item among paddlers, swimmers or skindivers and the helmsman must always bear this in mind. It is by no means unheard-of for people in the water to be seriously injured by an outboard's propeller. Nasty things happen if long hair, or even a tie or scarf, get caught in the rotating flywheel of a motor. This is obviously relevant to those outboards with exposed flywheels, but it can also happen if the hood is taken off an enclosed motor and one leans over to inspect something while it is running.

Before a motor is worked on, it is a good idea to pull off the sparkplug leads to prevent accidental starting. It can lead to a nasty accident if the motor happens not to be clamped to something solid—for instance if someone is merely holding it upright —or if one is thrown off balance while in the boat.

Fuel

The most important single aspect of looking after two-stroke outboards is in feeding them the correct grade of fuel and the correct oil mixed in the correct ratio. Recommendations for your particular outboard will be found in the owner's handbook or on the motor itself. Regular grade leaded gasoline is suitable for most outboards; only racing models need higher octane fuel.

Where gasoline is sold in a non-leaded form, refer to the makers or agent for the suitable grade, which should also be specified in the handbook. Two-stroke motors are less sensitive to the anti-knock properties of gasoline than cars, so one can happily use a low quality grade. Top grade fuel will not make a standard outboard perform any better, and will be a sheer waste of money. Four-strokes will also work well on the same lower grades because they have lower compression ratios than most modern car engines.

The lubricating oil used in cars makes a very poor outboard motor oil and should never be used. Even two-stroke self-mixing oils used in motorbikes and lawnmowers should not be used in high-performance (50:1 mix) water cooled outboards. For these, which are in fact most of the popular makes (Johnson, Evinrude, Chrysler, Mercury *et al.*), one should only use outboard motor oil, a special oil to OMC 381 and BIA TC–W (two-cycle water cooled) specification. Called outboard oils, they are easily available: Shell, Gulf, Mobile, Texaco, Valvoline, Mercury, OMC and Chrysler market them. They usually contain a dye so that fuel which has been treated with the oil is easily identified, and come in graduated plastic containers to simplify mixing. These oils are also suitable for water cooled motors that use a richer mixture than 50:1, but it is cheaper to use a self-mixing motorbike type oil from a garage, *provided* that this is what the makers recommend. (Seagull owners are specifically warned against outboard oils and recommended to use normal two-stroke oils.) Such two-stroke oils usually have the suffix "2-T" or "two-stroke," for example Shell (2-T).

If stuck without either outboard oil or two-stroke oil, then for as short a period as possible one can use a non-multigrade, non-additive, straight SAE 30 old-fashioned car engine oil. The significance of using the correct oil will be clearer after considering the following.

In a four-stroke engine such as a car engine, the moving parts are lubricated by a sump and pump system; only a small quantity of oil actually gets into the cylinder and is burned. The oil must run freely in ambient temperatures ranging from summer to winter (hence the multigrade oils) and it must successfully hold dirt and deposits in suspension (hence additives or high-detergency). In contrast, the oil fed into a two-stroke engine as part of the fuel/oil mix must pass *through* the combustion chamber after it has done its job of lubricating the crankcase and piston, leaving as little ash and carbon as possible. The additives used in car engine oils will burn inside the combustion chamber of a two-stroke leaving deposits which may cause pre-ignition, piston burning and cylinder wall scoring. Generally, piston temperatures are higher in a two-stroke than in a four-stroke, so the oil also has to be more chemically stable.

It can be seen that a good oil for a two-stroke is quite different from car engine oil, and various well-publicized tests have been done to show the effects of using the right and wrong oils. Outboards have been run in identical conditions for the same time but fed different oils; their pistons are examined after a running time of 100 hours. With car engine oil, thick carbon collects on the top, deposits form on the piston skirt, and the rings are stuck with gum and varnish. This situation is not quite so bad when two-stroke oils are used, but with the outboard oils the piston appears almost like new. The simple conclusion is that only the ignorant or the fool will use anything else in his high-performance 50:1 water cooled outboard when the maker specifically states that outboard oil must be used.

Deciding on the quantity of oil to add to the gasoline can be baffling when handbooks start talking about X ounces of oil to Y gallons of gas—what do you do if the tank only holds two-thirds of a gallon, carry a slide rule around? Even if the ratio is expressed as so many fractions of pints to a gallon, how can one accurately measure the small quantity of oil? With a 50:1 outboard oil container it is relatively straightforward using the graduated markings, although to get some degree of accuracy it is better to mix at least one gallon quantities in a separate container and then use this supply to fill the motor's small attached tank. A remote tank makes life easier.

If you always keep the *ratio* in mind (rather than pints to a gallon, for example) it is not too difficult to work out the proportions for any quantity or for metric units. There are 8 pints to a gallon, so a ratio of say 25:1 means that one needs 1/25th of a gallon of oil to every gallon of gasoline, i.e. 8/25ths of a pint which is about ⅓ of a pint. In metric units it is easier: there are 1000 cc to a liter; a 25::1 mixture would require 1000/25 cc of oil to each liter of gasoline, i.e. 40 cc.

Make sure the fuel container is clean and dry, otherwise you will have constant trouble from dirt or water in the carburetor. Shake the can after mixing whether the oil is self-mixing or outboard oil. It is best to pour in the oil first and then add the gasoline. In warm weather too much shaking is unnecessary and will cause fumes to come out of the breather hole. With a tank built into the boat add the oil slowly at the same time as the gasoline, if the fuel has to be mixed in the tank.

A fact that many people must be unaware of is that fuel goes stale after a few months. Cracked gasoline contains ingredients which form gum when stored for any length of time, leading to blocked pipes and carburetor troubles. While a motor is in regular use there is no problem, but during the winter lay-up the residual fuel can go stale. The simple answer is to drain the carburetor, fuel lines and tank. Rather than throwing fuel mixture away, it can be added in *small* quantities to the almost full tank of your car so that the oil is well diluted. There are fuel stabilizers which can be added to stop the deterioration for about a year—OMC 2 + 4 for instance.

Changes in the gasoline or oil you use may well have an effect on the running of the motor, necessitating slow-speed jet adjustment. Two-strokes are sensitive to changes in fuel so it is best to stick to a particular brand if possible. Generally speaking, additives claiming to have friction-reducing effects or tune-ups should be avoided. Like using high-octane fuel, the only effect is on your pocket. Just stick to the mixture recommended in the handbook.

Laying-up

Preservation of a motor over the winter prolongs its life considerably; left on the boat it will deteriorate badly. The least one should do is to store it ashore in the dry after washing it through and over with fresh water and squirting some oil into the cylinders through the sparkplug holes.

One of the advantages of an outboard is that one *can* take it home fairly easily, and having got it into the comfort of the garage one might as well do the preservation job properly and also do a bit of servicing so that at the beginning of the next season it is all ready for the water. To make working on the motor easier and prevent it getting knocks and scratches it is well worth making up a rough stand.

Usually the handbook gives a laying-up routine. Some outboard dealers offer a winterization plan including a service, but at a price, of course. The actual winterization is an easy do-it-yourself job, whereas some aspects of the service are not. A typical procedure for preservation would be:

1. Put the motor in fresh, clean water and start it up. Running at a fast tick-over, inject preserving oil into the carburetor intake at an increasing rate until the motor chokes and stalls.

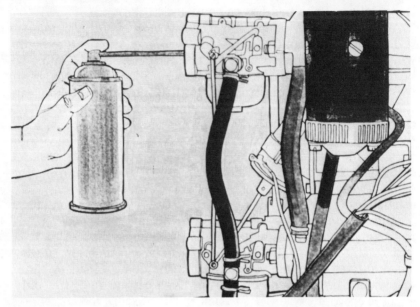

First, run the engine at about half-throttle in a fresh water tank until the cooling system is thoroughly flushed. Then squirt lubricant into the carburetor air intake slowly, at increasing volume until the engine stalls.

2. Wash off the exterior with fresh water, especially the tight nooks and angles, and put the motor on its storage stand.

3. Drain the carburetor, fuel line and tank (leave the cap screwed on the tank).

4. Disconnect the sparkplugs and rotate the engine to expel water in the pump. Leave the piston halfway up the cylinder: the ports will then be shut off by the side of the piston.

5. Wipe over with an oily rag; use an oily toothbrush for in-accessible places.

6. Store the motor in a dry, well-ventilated place.

Running in fresh water may be easier said than done. One can use a barrel, oildrum or other suitable water tub with the motor mounted on a makeshift but strong bracket at the correct height. (Sometimes fishing or sailing clubs rig these up for their members.) The gear lever should be in neutral. The object is to simultaneously swill out the cooling system and inject the preserving oil into the carburetor intake while the engine is running. Swilling-out can be done without running the motor, by using a garden hose and an inlet adapter available for some makes, but injecting oil into the cylinders through the plug

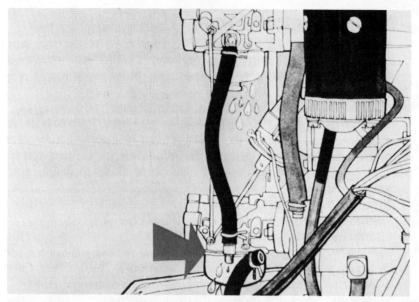

Next, lift the outboard from the tank and drain all the fuel from it by disconnecting all fuel lines and carburetor lines, and by removing the drain plugs from the carburetor and fuel pump. Also, drain the fuel tank and fog its inside with oil.

holes and then turning the engine over a few times is not so good because the crankcase may not be lubricated. Preserving oil is usually available from outboard dealers.

Rotate the engine by hand to empty the pump of water, but first to be sure to disconnect the plugs. Then remove the sparkplugs and either clean or replace them.

A typical servicing sequence during lay-up is as follows:

1. Swill out the tank through the filler cap; clean the fuel pump filter and/or carburetor filter.
2. Clean/replace and gap the sparking plug(s); screw them back in place.
3. Clean/replace and gap the contact breakers.
4. Inspect the high-tension plug leads for cracks. Renew if at all doubtful.
5. Grease up the steering and tilt pivots, clamp screws, throttle linkages, choke linkages and any other exposed pivots and locking devices.
6. Drain and refill the gearcase.
7. Remove the propeller and grease the propeller shaft.
8. Carefully dress up the propeller blade edges with a fine file if necessary, and touch up any scratches on the whole motor with paint supplied by a dealer. Make sure the surfaces are salt-free, clean and keyed by sandpapering before painting.
9. Generally check for loose nuts or damaged parts. Check the starter cord for fraying, and the fuel pipe connectors.

It is also worth considering any bits and pieces associated with the outboard—remote controls, the battery, lights, instruments and other electrical gear. If it is awkward to take them off the boat at least make sure that they are protected from wet and theft. The battery must be taken home and trickle-charged every month for a few hours, otherwise it may well discharge itself, sulphate and be a ruin at the beginning of the next season. Keep the acid level topped up with distilled water and the top clean.

Commissioning at the start of the season is easy if the motor has been preserved and serviced. The preserving oil will burn off very quickly once the engine has been started, but it is well to clean the plugs after an hour, or use old plugs for this first hour. Use fresh fuel. As soon as the engine has started, check that the cooling water is flowing through.

Motor overboard!

Assuming it is retrieved, quick action is essential. Salt water rapidly plays havoc with internal metal bearing surfaces: leaving the motor for the dealer on Monday morning may well wreck it. The best thing is to get it started as quickly as possible after getting rid of water in the cylinder and fuel system. Take out the sparkplug, lay the motor with the plug hole

Whether you keep the sparkplugs or replace with new ones, check the gap with a feeler gauge to see if the distance conforms to the maker's specifications.

Don't forget to clean or replace the fuel filters, located at the fuel pump or carburetor or both. Excessive filtrate should prompt a search for its source, or eventual damage will result.

An outboard drowned in saltwater has to be drowned again in fresh, and the sooner the better. Carburetors must be removed, cleaned, and completely dried.

downwards, and turn it over many times. Then drain the carburetor and fuel line (and tank if that got wet too). Pump up fresh fuel, put in the sparkplug, and try to start the motor on the back of a boat or in a tank of water. If it won't start check that the plug gap is not wet with water, and if it still will not start take off the flywheel and dry off the ignition (a fan heater or hair dryer is ideal). If all else fails, get the motor to a dealer, ideally within about three hours of taking it out of the water. If this is not possible, some makers—Johnson, for instance—recommend that the motor be *re-submerged* in *fresh* water to avoid exposure to air. An alternative is to fill up the cylinder and crankcase with oil, after any water has been drained out. If the engine *can* be started, run it for at least half an hour. In any case the handbook should be consulted, and usually dealer attention is specified whether the motor re-started or not. The important thing is that either the motor is re-started immediately *or* it is taken to a dealer within a few hours of immersion (and that the dealer takes action immediately).

If the motor was running when it went in, it may be that water entered the cylinder and created a hydraulic lock, dam-

Ignition components should be soaked in freshwater, then dried with compressed air. For final drying, bake in 225° oven for two hours.

aging the piston rod or crankshaft. Turning the engine over slowly by the flywheel should establish any binding, indicating damage. After being in salt water, even if the engine is success-fully re-started it is necessary to clean out the salt particles from places like the magneto fairly soon, otherwise severe corrosion and poor running are likely to result.

Temperamental motors

Poor running or failure to start *should* be traceable to a spe-cific mechanical or electrical fault, and yet on many occasions one hears owners of outboards (or indeed any type of engine) relating how no actual defect could be found (plugs, fuel, carb jets, contact breakers, etc.), but that suddenly the motor started and ran normally. This is the sort of thing I call temper-ament. While not suggesting that a mechanical object can have a mind and will of its own (there must be *something* wrong that you did not spot), an internal combustion engine working on the principles of fuel/air carburetion, crankcase induction and electric ignition is subject to a large number of variables each dictating the level of performance. The carburetor is a simple

137

and cheap device with which to mix air and fuel, but it is by no means ideal. Most two-strokes use crankcase compression for induction, so the fuel/air vapor has to go via the crankcase to the cylinder rather than directly as in a four-stroke. This is one feature which causes temperament. Electric ignition has its failings, and most car breakdowns are due to ignition problems; on the water the ignition has to contend with damp and salt air. It is a great shame that diesel engines cannot be made light and economically enough to use as outboards: the fuel is injected directly into the cylinder and ignited by sheer compression without either electrical ignition or a carburetor.

Temperament has a great deal to do with the following parts, so regular attention to them pays off handsomely in future reliability:

sparkplug (s)
contact breaker (s)
fuel filter (s)
float chamber
carburetor jets

And just as important, be sure of the fuel—fresh, clean, and with the correct oil in the correct ratio.

Quick and Easy Maintenance

The heading should stress "simple," partly because it is that kind of maintenance which counts so much towards motor reliability and life, and partly because repairs within the powerhead or leg are beyond most of us, because of lack of mechanical skill or special tools. Sophisticated motors, especially in the larger powers, really do need specialized knowledge and tools; smaller ones under about 8 hp are generally a lot simpler and easier to work on. A few, like the Seagull are actually designed for easy repair and maintenance.

A book of this small size cannot be a substitute for a manual for your particular motor; it can only give hints and general guidance. Even for the simplest work on any outboard it is essential to get some data from the manufacturers: owners' handbooks tend to be rather basic and may not tell you such things as how to take the flywheel off to get at the contact breakers. The full workshop manual is usually a forbidding-looking tome, and there may be some reluctance on the part of the agent or dealer to sell you one (in the case of larger sophisticated motors) on the grounds that the motor may ultimately end up at the dealer's in an even worse state. (While a motor is under warranty, any amateur repairs will invariably invalidate the warranty.) At a level between the shop manual and the owner's handbook, there may be a service guide booklet available (e.g. Mercury) giving the nitty-gritty information and concise instructions without delving into such things as crankshaft assembly. Other detailed, illustrated do-it-yourself manuals such as the Glenn's series are published as books, and widely available.

Some parts of any motor gradually wear out and eventually cause it to fail. Maintenance catches this process before too much wear has taken place, hence reliability is achieved. To this end, one can draw up a list of maintenance jobs.

1. Gearcase oil: check level and for water contamination half-way through season; renew at end of season.
2. Greasing: at the end of season and halfway through.
3. Fuel filters, tank: clean at end of season.
4. Sparkplug (s) : renew each season (don't clean them); with 50:1 mix and CD ignition renew every other season.
5. Contact breakers: hone and gap once a year. Fit new ones every two or three years and at the same time check timing.
6. HT leads to plugs: clean every year and replace after three or four years.
7. Carb float chamber, jets: clean every season—not really necessary if fuel is drained in winter and filters are habitually clean when inspected.
8. Battery: top up every month with distilled water only.

The times mentioned are appropriate for normal pleasure boating (around 100 hours' running in a six month season) with the motor being laid up in the winter. Indeed it is during laying-up that most of these jobs are best done. One item that is missing from the list is the water pump: the flexible impeller gradually wears out and the only way to check it is to dismantle the leg, not an easy job. Ideally one should check it yearly and replace if necessary (and maybe the impeller housing, if it's worn). Carburetor adjustments should only rarely be necessary. Decarbonizing is a rare necessity nowadays, especially if the correct fuel mixture has been used. Sparkplugs are perhaps the most common things that have to be touched: they are so often the cause of poor running that in the above list I suggested renewal every season as a matter of course. Cleaning often makes the plug no better, and the cost of new plugs is really relatively insignificant. HT leads can also be a cause of mystifying faults; the insulation ages, and even the slightest crack can cause trouble, hence renewal every few years. The frequency of carburetor cleaning depends largely on the cleanliness of the fuel that is put into the tank, routine swilling out of all dirt, water or sludge in the tank, and the efficiency of the filters.

Sparkplugs

Difficult starting and general poor running can often be tracked down to simply a faulty sparkplug. There may appear to be nothing wrong, but the insulator may have a tiny crack in a place you cannot see. More commonly the plug gap is incor-

Surface gap plugs should not be cleaned—the ignition system has enough voltage to jump a dirty gap. Replace when the center electrode is down 1/32 inch.

rectly set, and some engines are particularly sensitive to this. Plugs do have a limited life, and it is better to replace them at regular intervals than wait until they let you down.

Before fitting a new plug set it to the specified gap (stated in the manual) by bending the side electrode: just because they are new does not mean that they are set properly. There is usually a metal gasket which ensures a good seal in the cylinder providing the plug is not tightened too much. The torque to use will be found in the manual (usually 20 pound feet (2.8 kg/m) with 14 mm plugs), but if you have no torque wrench there may be an instruction to tighten finger-tight plus one quarter-turn with a wrench. Overtightening may also damage the thread in the cylinder head. It is well to clean around the plug where it seats in the cylinder head *before* taking the plug out, to prevent bits of dirt falling through the hole; wipe the perimeter of the hole clean with a fingertip before fitting a new plug. Avoid putting any force on the porcelain insulator when using a plug socket or wrench: this is the delicate part of the plug and vital to its performance and life.

141

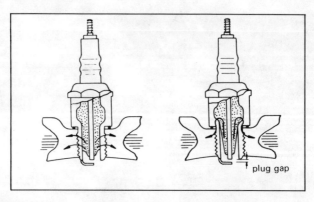

Hot and cold plugs. The shape of the ceramic insulator dictates the length of heat path, and thus how fast heat is taken away from the tip.

It is most important to use plugs of the specified size and reach—the length of the threaded part—as the tip of the plug should just protrude into the combustion chamber. They also vary in heat range. Hot plugs are designed so that the tips run hotter, the conduction of heat away from the tip being impeded by having it travel farther down the plug before passing into the metal body and hence the cooler cylinder head. Cold plugs run cooler. The handbook will specify the type of plug that has the correct heat range for average use, but it may be advantageous after some experience with the motor to choose a hotter or a cooler plug. A hotter plug will help to reduce the fouling rate by burning off carbon. On the other hand, if the motor is used on a very light and fast speedboat and the propeller size allows full-throttle revs at the top end of the rev range, a colder plug may be necessary to avoid pre-ignition or a short life through overheating.

One can tell whether the plugs are suitable by taking them out after half a season and inspecting the ends. They should be clean and not burned, and light brown or grey in color. If they are black and sooty they are too cold: fit a hotter plug. A hard white deposit means they are running too hot: fit colder ones. Before changing to a hotter or colder type first be absolutely sure that the plug condition is not due to faulty engine tuning. Sooty plugs can be caused by too much oil in the fuel mixture, a hole in the fuel pump diaphragm, or a choke that is not opening fully. White deposits can be formed by ignition timing that is too far advanced, or by overheating due to a cooling system fault or a weak jet setting. The wrong lubricating oil will also form deposits on the plugs. Deposits of aluminum on the plugs probably means that the piston is being burned, and this should be immediately investigated before serious damage is done.

Having satisfied yourself that the engine is in good condition and the fuel correct, a sensible choice of slightly hotter or slightly colder plugs than normally recommended can be made. Sparkplug manufacturers offer different heat ratings for each plug size and reach, and charts are available to relate equivalent plugs from different manufacturers.

Plugs cannot be cleaned very satisfactorily by hand, even with emery paper or a tiny file. Grit blasting in the type of machines that garages use is better, but in view of the small running time of a pleasure boat motor and the low cost of plugs it is best to renew them regularly. It is worth keeping the outside of the insulator clean. Oil collects dirt, and dirt attracts damp which can provide a leakage path for the high-tension current, causing poor starting and misfiring. Surface gap plugs generally last longer, and should *not* be cleaned. The CD ignition systems associated with surface gap plugs can produce enough voltage to spark easily across a dirty gap. If the center electrode is burned down by more than about $\frac{3}{32}$ inches (0.8 mm) or if the insulator is cracked, the plug should be replaced.

Gear oil and greasing

Regular renewal of gearcase oil is essential to the long life of the gears. This is especially true on the larger motors as the high powers being transmitted create very high pressures on the relatively small gear teeth. Any old oil will *not* do; even an EP 90 gear oil is often not recommended, so stick to the makers' specification, which should be found in the handbook. Most gearcase troubles are directly attributable to the use of the wrong oil.

The usual recommendation is that the oil level is checked, or the oil changed, after the motor has run for the first ten hours or so. Thereafter the level should be checked every thirty or so hours, and the oil changed every hundred hours' running or every season whichever comes first. The only accurate way of counting the hours run is to fit an hour meter, which is an electric clock that only runs when the motor is running, but it is an expensive little item. One can always think back and add up how much running is done each week and multiply this by the number of weeks in the season. Usually one finds that this comes to less than a hundred hours a season, so gearcase lubrication turns out to be an oil change at the end of the season and a check on the level halfway through.

Most motors have a gearcase drain plug and a level plug. The oil is rather thick and drains more easily if both plugs are taken out and the ambient temperature warm rather than cold. The motor should be upright when the operation is done since the top plug is a level plug, i.e. the oil should come up to this hole. Refilling is best done by injecting the oil through the lower plug hole, thus allowing the air inside the gearcase to escape through the level plug hole. When oil appears at the level hole, the level plug is screwed in so that very little oil is lost when the nozzle of the oil container is taken away from the lower hole (outboard gear oil is sold in special containers for this purpose). If the case is filled via the upper hole air can get trapped around the parts inside the case, giving a false oil level. If filling *is* done this way, then leave the motor for half an hour to allow all the air to come out, and then top up to the level hole again. Fit new washers to the plugs if the old ones are in any way damaged.

When checking the oil level (topping up if necessary) it is worth looking for water contamination at the same time. If

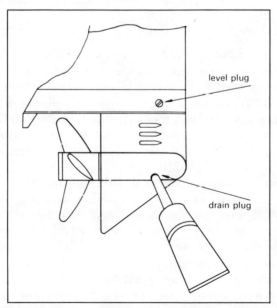

Refilling the gearcase with outboard gear oil.

water does get into the gearcase (probably through a worn propeller shaft seal) it does the gears no good at all. After the engine has been standing for some time, or overnight, remove the lower plug and any water will come out first. Don't do this immediately after the engine has been running because the oil and water will be mixed. If there is water, the leak must be repaired very soon otherwise gear damage may result.

There are usually grease nipples for such things as the steering pivot and tilt pivot bearings; a grease gun must be used for these. Clamp screws, throttle and choke linkages (including the linkages to the magneto), the gear lever shaft, motor cover latch and tilt lever shaft also need greasing. The grease is put on straight from the tube; there are special outboard greases available from dealers. The recommended period is usually every month in salt water and every sixty days in fresh water, but obviously commonsense can be used depending on the conditions. For a motor normally stowed in a dry garage and only used in fresh water, the periods between greasing can be much longer.

Safeguarding your propeller

There are basically two methods by which a propeller is mounted on its shaft. It may fit on to a plain shaft with the

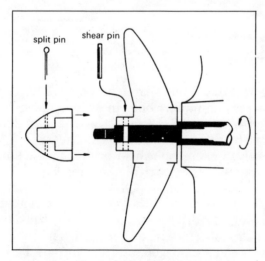

One of the many detail variations of securing the propeller by means of a shear pin.

drive transmitted by a shear pin passing through a hole drilled right through the propeller boss and shaft. In the event of the propeller striking something solid the pin shears before any serious damage is done to either it or the transmission. The shear pin has to be replaced before the motor can be used again,

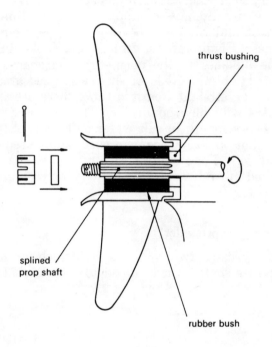

thrust bushing

splined
prop shaft

rubber bush

A rubber bush instead of a shear pin absorbs shocks.

so it is wise to carry a few spares on board. They must be the correct ones for the motor; only in an emergency should you use a piece of wire or nail, because the degree of shock protection is affected by the size and material of the pin.

Alternatively, a neoprene rubber bush is pressed into the propeller hub and the inner part of the propeller hub slides into place along splines on the propeller shaft. The rubber bush allows slippage to take place if the propeller hits something hard, but will take up the drive again afterwards, thus avoiding the bother and delay of renewing a shear pin. The rubber bush can itself age or become damaged, and it can only be replaced by a dealer or propeller specialist. It is tested by setting the propeller in a vice and checking the torque required to make it slip.

After removing the propeller for service or storage, lubricate the prop shaft and nuts with water resistant grease to prevent corrosion lock.

The propeller is prevented from sliding up and down the shaft by a collar between it and the gearcase bearing, and by a nut on the end of the shaft. The nut may be in the form of a cone, but is prevented from unscrewing by a split-pin or tab washer. Whenever the propeller is refitted it is vital to bend over the split-pin or tabs otherwise it will probably fall off. Bending can only be done two or three times; if in doubt fit a new pin or washer. There may be other washers or rubber rings in the assembly, so watch out for them, especially if you are working over the water, and replace them in the original sequence.

Grease the propeller shaft and nuts with a water resistant grease so that corrosion does not lock the whole assembly solid

147

before the next dismantling. Jam a piece of wood between a blade and the underside of the cavitation plate to stop the propeller rotating, if the nut is difficult to undo. Stuck pins can be tapped out with another pin or a nail.

A bent or badly chipped propeller will be unbalanced and may cause premature wear of the shaft bearings and oil seals. Major damage can only be repaired by propeller specialists, but small nicks or burrs can be filed clean. Preserve the shape of the edges of the blades; not that the after face of each blade is flat while the other is rounded. Touch up with paint afterwards.

Fuel system

Where an outboard has an integral tank the fuel feed to the carburetor is by gravity. With a remote tank a pump on the engine sucks up fuel even if the tank happens to be well below the level of the carburetor. To fill the feed pipes and carburetor

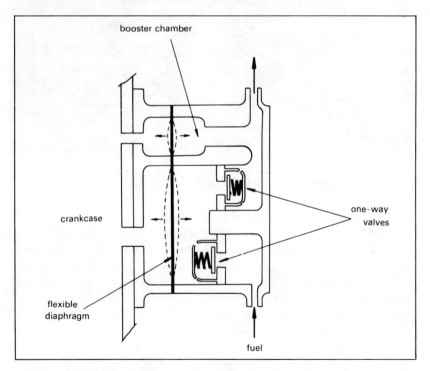

A typical fuel pump, operated by pressure variations in the crankcase. A filter may be incorporated.

initially, a hand squeeze pump is fitted in the line; as soon as the engine starts, its automatic pump takes over. This pump has a flexible diaphragm open to the fluctuating pressure in the crankcase. Each time the piston ascends, the crankcase suction acts on the diaphragm, which sucks a small quantity of fuel from the tank; valves stop it draining back.

A carburetor is simply a device which mixes fuel with air to form an explosive mixture. The ratio of fuel to air is critical; for idling it should be about 1:8, at high revs about 1:12. The fuel is sucked through a small orifice (a jet) by the air on its way to the crankcase. To give the right mixture at different speeds two jets are usually fitted, a low speed jet and a high speed one. Most outboards now have a fixed, non-adjustable high speed jet which consists of a small brass plug with a fine hole down the middle. The slow speed jet is usually adjustable and consists of a needle projecting into a tapered hole. For cold starts a very rich mixture is required, provided by a choke. This is usually a butterfly valve which when closed almost blanks off the air intake, thus restricting the air flow. A constant fuel level inside the carburetor to feed the jets is provided by the float

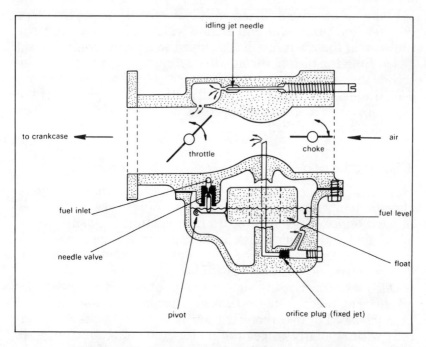

The ingeniously simple operation of the carburetor.

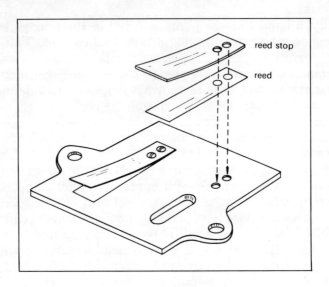

Reed or leaf valves to control the admission of the fuel/air mixture into the crankcase.

chamber, which works on the same principle as a lavatory cistern.

Many outboards are fitted with leaf valves, spring steel flaps between the carburetor and engine which only open when the pressure in the crankcase has dropped to a predetermined level (each time the piston ascends the cylinder). As the piston descends they shut and prevent the escape of the air/fuel mixture back through the carburetor. Small motors often make use of the piston to cover and uncover ports at the appropriate time, thus dispensing with valves.

Adjusting the jets

Different brands of fuel, changes in altitude or widely different climatic temperatures require different jet settings. In the case of fixed orifice jets the outboard manufacturers usually recommend that the standard jet is changed for a leaner one if the motor is to be operated several thousand feet above sea level (air being less dense at high altitudes).

Once set properly, the slow running jet should not need any adjustment unless some operating change occurs—a different gasoline or oil or decarbonizing for instance. If it has to be fiddled with regularly to get the motor running reasonably well, there could be dirt in the tank and fuel line continually blocking the jet orifice or the float chamber valve. Adjusting the jet is usually done with the engine thoroughly warm and idling. Screw the jet needle in (clockwise = leaner) until the motor starts to misfire or spit. Then turn it back anticlockwise (richer) until the motor slows down through the mixture being over-rich. The correct setting is roughly halfway between these extremes: the motor should run fast and smooth. It is better to be slightly on the rich rather than the lean side. The note of the engine as it slows and revs is the important thing to listen for; with multicylinder engines, especially those with multi-carburetors, the change in revs is difficult to detect and a tachometer is advisable. Depending on the motor, it may be better to run it idling *in gear* (in water, of course) while adjusting the slow speed jet. Do it whichever way gives the best result.

Adjusting the jet needle has nothing to do with setting the idling speed so that when gear is engaged the engine does not stall. The jet setting determines the mixture strength; to obtain the correct idling speed there is a stop on the throttle valve on the carburetor. Adjustment is usually by means of screw and locknut, or a screw and compression spring. The idling speed should be the slowest that the motor can run smoothly and yet not stall when put into gear. Too fast a speed will wear the clutch dogs prematurely. Ideally, a tachometer should be used to obtain the speed specified in the handbook—another reason for fitting such an instrument.

Adjustable high speed jets are set in the same manner but with the engine running at nearly full throttle. If for some reason the jet has got hopelessly out of adjustment, screw the needle fully home on its seat (but *gently*, otherwise you may score a groove on the needle) and then back off about one turn and proceed from there.

Motors with more than one carburetor are adjusted one carburetor at a time in the manner described. If detecting the change in note is difficult, then use a tachometer.

Cleaning the carburetor Dismantling a carburetor is usually a simple job not requiring special tools. The places where dirt can cause trouble are the float chamber valve and the two jets. If dirt is found it is best to go upstream and locate its source in the fuel pump filter, fuel lines or tank, so that blockage does not happen again. Cleaning is best done with a gum solvent (obtainable from the dealer) and a small paint brush, not a rag because of the fluff which might be left to subsequently block the jets. It is wise to renew any gaskets which look doubtful, especially the one between the carburetor and the engine inlet manifold, because any air leaks there alter the mixture and can lead to all sorts of mystifying running troubles.

When cleaning the main jet plug squirt down the hole against a bright light and clean out any dirt with an air hose. Simply blowing down the jet *may* clear the blockage, particularly if a piece of plastic pipe is pushed over the end and the pipe put to the lips. The main jet plug is usually accessible without dismantling the carburetor.

Inspect the tips of adjustable jet needles, which should taper to a fine point; if there is a score mark around the tip then someone has been forcing the needle down onto its seat. In that case replace the needle, because the tip is very important to correct carburetion.

The float chamber valve should be inspected for wear, and the seal of the valve needle against its seat can be checked by blowing through the fuel inlet and gently lifting the float. The air flow should cut off at very gentle pressure before the float reaches the limit of its travel (remember, the lifting force is only due to the small buoyancy of the float). Replace the valve/ seat assembly if there is any doubt. Also, check that the needle does not stick in its seat and that the float is not full of fuel. Usually the float should cut off the flow when it lifts to the horizontal on its pivoted arm. If there is a filter at the carburetor this should be cleaned as well as the sump of the float chamber.

Where possible, cleaning should be done without taking the carburetor off the engine, as the controls and magneto linkage can then remain undisturbed. If it has to be taken off, choose a clean bench or table on which to do the dismantling. Complete cleaning and inspection need only be done very infrequently, depending on the cleanliness of the fuel supply and how the motor has been treated. At lay-up time I suggest that the filters be cleaned, together with the main jet, and the float chamber lid or lower bowl taken off and the chamber swilled out with solvent.

Fuel pump There is usually a fuel filter integral with the pump which should be periodically cleaned. The pump itself may be a non-serviceable unit which if it goes wrong has to be replaced. The things to check, if the pump is suspect, are the diaphragm and valves. If the diaphragm shows the slightest sign of wear or a pinhole it must be replaced. The slightest hole allows neat fuel to be sucked into the crankcase, resulting in

Take off the back of the carburetor housing to reach the fuel lines. While you're at it, inspect the gasket and replace if at all worn or cracked.

wet plugs and other troubles. To check the outlet valves blow through the outlet hole: you should be able to suck air through, but not blow. Check the inlet valve in the opposite way.

Reed valves   When a valve breaks or for some reason fails to seat properly, the engine runs badly and misses on one cylinder, and the blowback can sometimes be detected. The only course of action is to replace the reeds, which is not a very difficult or expensive job. The reeds should lie flat on their seats and be neither distorted nor cracked. If a reed is found to have broken off, search for the missing pieces, which may cause damage inside the engine (if they have not done so already). Very tiny pieces may be passed straight through into the exhaust.

Tank and hoses   Swill out any dirt and sludge from the tank once a year via the filler cap. There may be a special drain screw to fully drain the tank.

Hose connectors have O-ring seals which if damaged or worn allow air to enter the fuel line, causing the motor either to stop when idling or run badly at high speed. Thus it is worth checking these vital seals each year, and replacing them if they look worn. The plunger or ball is pushed off the O-ring and the seal itself hooked out. The new ring should be smeared with oil to prevent damage while being inserted. Check also for cracks in the primer bulb and fuel hose.

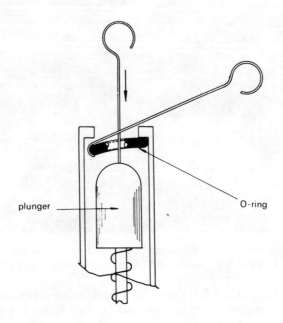

plunger

O-ring

Hooking out the O-ring seal from a fuel hose connector using tools made from $\frac{1}{16}$-inch (1.5 mm) wire.

Ignition system

Several types of ignition systems are used on current outboards, the simplest being a self-contained magneto under the flywheel, consisting of a coil, condenser and contact breakers. The system is independent of a battery. The larger motors, on which hand starting would be too heavy and electric starting is standard, have battery ignition as on a car. Some multi-cylinder motors have a separate bolted-on, toothed, belt-driven magneto containing a car-type distributor. CD (capacitor discharge) ignition comes with or without contact breakers, and may or may not be dependent on a battery for the initial electric supply. Because a magneto does not provide current unless the engine is running, lights or instruments run off it will not work when the engine is stopped, whereas battery current is available at any time. Apart from breakdown, one can think of a number of likely circumstances when power might be needed without propulsion.

Except for breakerless CD ignition, the one item that is common to all systems, and needs regular attention, is the contact breaker. Many multi-cylinder engines have two contact breakers fitted. Where a belt-driven magneto is employed, the contact breakers are usually readily accessible by taking off the distributor cap, but where they are under a flywheel it usually has to come off. Some motors have windows in the flywheel through which one can just about clean and adjust the points. Since the flywheel is pressed down on a taper on the crankshaft by its retaining nut, a quite considerable pull-off force is needed. Simply levering the edge of the flywheel will probably lead to damage, and the only recommended way is to use an extracting tool. On some engines one can overcome the friction of the taper by having one person lifting the motor by the flywheel and another person hitting the retaining nut sharply with a hammer, after slackening the retaining nut about two turns. This is the recommended practice on many smaller motors, e.g. Seagulls. Hitting the nut *too* hard may damage the bearings. If you are intending to service the engine yourself, then taking the flywheel off will be a regular job, so it is well to make up an extracting tool or get the maker's special tool.

The condition of the contact breaker points is vital to the good running of the motor. They should open to a certain gap as the engine is rotated; the handbook will tell you the actual

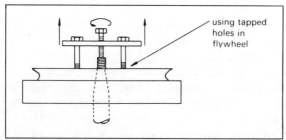

using tapped holes in flywheel

Pulling off a flywheel. There are often tapped holes in the top of the flywheel for this purpose. The object is to get a straight pull up on the flywheel, while pushing down on the top of the crankshaft. A sharp tap with a hammer helps. Special extractors are usually available from dealers, or it is not too difficult to make one from thick steel plate and two or three bolts into tapped holes in the flywheel.

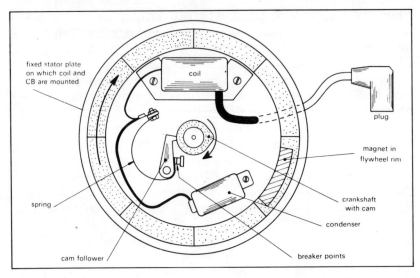

A simple flywheel magneto. As it skims past the coil with its steel laminations, the magnet in the rotating flywheel rim generates current in the primary part of the coil which passes to the contact breaker (CB) points via the spring. The points are held shut by the spring until the cam comes round and suddenly lifts the cam follower, thus opening the points. The sudden cessation of current creates a large voltage in the secondary part of the coil which passes to the plug and causes a spark. Note that the end of the spring is held on a post but must be insulated from it, as must the leads from the coil and the condenser. The condenser creates a reservoir of current and is there mainly to reduce sparking across the points and consequent rapid pitting. It can be tested with a battery and light bulb: current should not pass through.

gap, which varies with the make. The points should meet squarely and the surfaces be smooth, clean and free of pits. The tiniest bit of dirt or oil on the points can cause an intermittent or weak spark. Wipe them clean with a fluff-free rag and a spot of neat gasoline, and hone them with a fine grinding stone (not a file). Rapid pitting over a running time of only a few hours may indicate that the condenser is faulty. Both it and the contact breakers *should* be inexpensive to replace, and it is not worth being miserly. The fiber tip of the cam follower gradually wears, especially when new, and so the breaker gap gradually reduces (when new, set it at about 0.002 inches greater than normal). A spot of grease on the cam helps, though there is usually an oil-filled cam wick. Make sure the interior of the whole of the magneto is dry, clean and free of oil.

Adjusting the breaker gap is usually a fiddly and rather hit-and-miss affair. The engine is turned until the cam follower

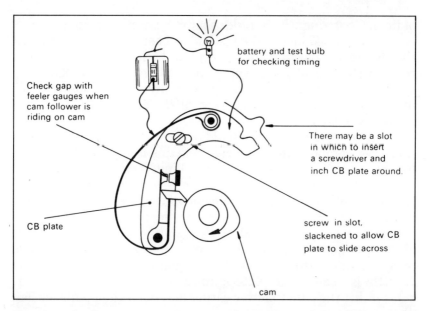

Gapping the points, and using a test lamp and battery to check the ignition timing.

is at the highest point of the cam and the points are therefore open. There is usually a screw in a slotted hole which when slackened allows the contact breaker on its own mounting plate to be shifted slightly until the gap is correct (as tested by a feeler gauge). Shifting the plate is best done by levering the tip of a screwdriver against a fixed part of the magneto; there may be a slot for just this purpose. Tighten up the screw and test the gap again with clean feeler gauges. Replacing contact breakers is usually straightforward. For one thing, the actual points, spring and cam follower come as one unit. The spring part is electrically insulated from the baseplate but connected to one or two wires. Bearing this in mind, replace the contact breakers in exactly the same way as they were dismantled—indeed take a note of the sequence of the bits as they disassemble.

Ignition coils sometimes age or short-circuit themselves. If the spark is weak and neither the points nor the high-tension lead nor the condenser are at fault, replace the coil—again, this is usually not difficult or too expensive.

Timing Combustion is not instantaneous when the spark ignites the mixture, but takes a finite though very small amount

157

of time. Consequently, in order that maximum combustion pressure is developed before the piston has been driven too far down the cylinder, sparking must occur a little before the piston reaches the top of its travel (top dead center or TDC). The spark is thus timed to occur at so many degree before TDC, degrees meaning the angular turn of the crankshaft. This timing is obviously important.

At higher revs the spark should occur earlier, because the time taken for combustion to develop remains much the same as at low revs, while the piston is travelling faster. Whereas slow running calls for a timing of only a few degrees before TDC, full throttle may require it to be advanced by 30° or so. Small motors often do not have the sophistication of automatic retard/advance devices to alter the ignition timing as the revs change; larger motors usually have a linkage from the throttle lever on the carburetor to the magneto stator plate. As the throttle is opened the plate is rotated, causing the crankshaft cams to lift the cam follower earlier and open the points earlier. This system is in contrast to that on most car engines, where usually both a vacuum system and centrifugal weights in the distributor alter the timing.

On most outboards there is no manual knob for fine timing, which is done by adjusting the points gap. If the gap is correct the slow running timing should be correct: what is more important is that the higher speed timing should also be correct. One can look at the timing question with the assumption that if the contact breaker gap is correct then the timing should be correct, providing the carburetor/stator plate linkage has not been disturbed.

To check that the points open at the specified precise moment before TDC, it is too inexact to turn the crankshaft slowly and merely watch for the gap to open: one can be several degrees out. A simple and much more effective way is to connect up a test bulb and battery across the points so that as the engine is slowly turned the light will go on and off as the points close and open repeatedly. The motor must be turned in the direction of its normal rotation—do not go past the position at which the points open, and then back—and continue round a complete revolution. Turning back may damage the water pump impeller by bending its vanes backwards.

Judging the degree of rotation of the crankshaft is often not as easy as on a car, where timing marks are usually scribed on to the flywheel or a pulley. To get at the points on an outboard the flywheel usually has to be taken off first. One can get a timing mark either by inserting a probe into the cylinder through the sparkplug hole and feeling the movement of the piston, or by mounting a pointer on the protruding end of the crankshaft. With the first method one must know the distance that the piston should be below TDC corresponding to the number of degrees before TDC. If this method is recommended, a special probe tool is usually available; it may take the form of a dial gauge with a sparkplug thread. The other method also means a special pointer, but one can be simply made up with wire or a strip of aluminum held on to the end of the crankshaft by the flywheel nut. A mark is then put on the edge of the stator plate for TDC. If this method of timing is advocated in the handbook, there will probably be marks already there, including the maximum spark advance position. In multi-cylinder engines the timing is usually referred to the topmost (no. 1) cylinder.

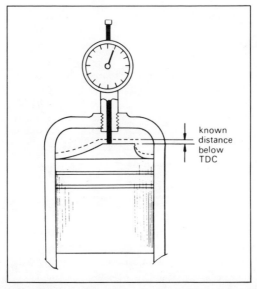

known
distance
below
TDC

If the ignition timing is specified as a certain known distance before the piston reaches TDC, the following is the procedure for checking the timing. The gauge is zeroed when the piston is at TDC, and then the engine is turned until the piston is the specified distance lower down. The measurement must be made accurately because an error of more than a few thousands of an inch will lead to the timing being several degrees out (an engineer's dial gauge gives enough accuracy). This method is best used for the maximum spark advance timing, not the idling speed timing where the distance below TDC will be very small and accuracy more difficult.

The same procedures can be used to check the maximum spark advance. The throttle is opened wide to advance the stator plate fully, and again the engine is slowly turned until the contact breaker just opens, at which point the pistons should be at the specified distance before TDC (or the crankshaft so many degrees before TDC). If the timing is not correct, the linkage from the throttle to the magneto is adjusted in length, usually by a screw and locknut arrangement.

A stroboscopic timing light makes the job of checking the timing much easier. This is a light which is connected into the HT circuit to one plug and flashes every time there is a spark at that plug. With the engine running, the timing light is pointed at the rotating flywheel and any marks appear stationary to the eye. The larger engines, particularly those with CD ignition, have a timing scale scribed around the perimeter

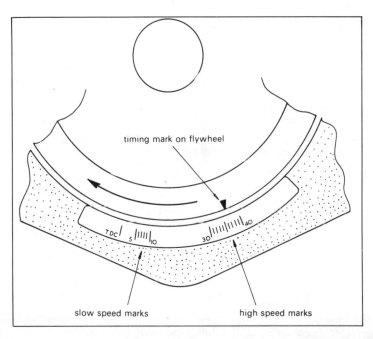

Clear timing marks which make checking the timing with a strobe light very easy. The marks are normally associated with no. 1 cylinder. Without a strobe light one can take the flywheel off, fit a test tube across the points, and fix a wire or stiff pointer to the end of the crankshaft using the flywheel nut. Set the engine at TDC (by sensing the movement of the piston through the sparkplug hole) and set the pointer to the TDC mark; then carry out the normal procedure for checking the timing. This is an accurate method.

of the flywheel or some stationary part of the engine for just this purpose, and on breakerless CD ignition engines the timing light method is often the only way to check the timing.

Twin contact breakers On multi-cylinder engines one often finds two sets of contact breakers underneath the flywheel. In a twin cylinder engine, for instance, this avoids the need for a distributor; where one contact breaker serves more than one sparkplug it is usually necessary to have a distributor (as on a car) to switch the high voltage to the correct plug.

Both sets of contact breakers have to be set to the correct gap, and this should automatically make the timing correct so long as the throttle/stator plate linkage has not been disturbed. In any case, if no. 1 cylinder is timed to one set of points then the other set should be correct for the other cylinder. For the larger engines, makers often are more fussy about synchronization of the two sets of breakers, and the timing of both should be checked in order to achieve 100% engine performance. This is done by first setting the two gaps correctly, then timing one set to the maximum spark advance (open throttle) position, and finally making sure that the other set of points open at exactly 180° away (in the case of two cylinder engines). If they do not, the gap is altered slightly.

Distributors There are a few small points to look for: tracking across the distributor cap, corrosion and dirt, and the little central carbon brush with its spring. The carbon brush should depress easily against the spring and not be worn. High-voltage tracking is readily noticeable; it can cause misfiring because the high-tension current tracks to earth around the distributor cap rather than going to a sparkplug. If the cap cannot be cleaned up, or if it is cracked or doubtful in any way, it is best to replace it.

CD ignition If a CD system has contact breakers, the procedures for replacing and gapping them are the same as already described. Because the current flowing across the points is so very much less than on an ordinary magneto, they last much longer. On the other hand the cam follower wears just as much, so the gap will gradually reduce and must be readjusted as with simple magnetos.

Breakerless CD ignition has no moving parts to wear and the timing is fixed: providing the sensors and spark advance throttle linkage has not been disturbed, it should never need checking. The individual electrical parts of the CD ignition system are

161

generally sealed units—nonserviceable and repared by replacement. For the motor owner this means nil maintenance and repair (apart from the sparkplugs and leads), and, if trouble is suspected in the ignition system, testing the strength of the spark, which should jump a ½-inch gap (beware of electrical shock). It is often a stated requirement that the plug leads should never be left high and dry when taken off the plugs, otherwise the electrics can be damaged. If the plugs are taken out, reconnect the leads and lay the plugs on the engine block.

To work on the ignition or not? The larger the motor and the more cylinders it has, the more complicated the ignition system. If you are familiar with car ignition systems there should be no problem in learning how to deal with the simple magneto of small motors, right down to replacing the coils. CD ignition is easy to service, but you *must* have a workshop manual and the test equipment. Repair should be so rarely needed that it is better to take the motor to a service agent. It is the contact breaker that needs the attention, and it is relatively simple to maintain with simple tools. This brief description of how to go about the ignition system is only intended as an introduction to the subject; the maker's manual *must* be consulted if only to get the correct gap and timing.

Electrical system (other than the ignition)

The only maintenance of the charging and starting system concerns the battery. Its acid level should be checked monthly and topped up with distilled water, and the top and terminals kept dry and clean. The latter point is particularly important in the case of motors fitted with AC alternators rather than DC dynamos (generators), because if the terminals become so corroded that electrical continuity is lost then the rectifier may be damaged, depending on the design of the circuit. Damage may also result if the motor is used without a battery, or a wire forming part of the circuit vibrates loose or chafes on something, or the harness plug comes loose. The handbook will give the precautions, if any, to be observed.

Remember that battery acid eats holes in clothes, and be very careful not to splash any acid into your eyes. Copious clean water will wash away acid splashes, and baking soda (bicarbonate) will neutralize any remaining acid. Never add acid to a battery—only water. While being charged, lead/acid batteries give off hydrogen, which is an explosive gas but lighter

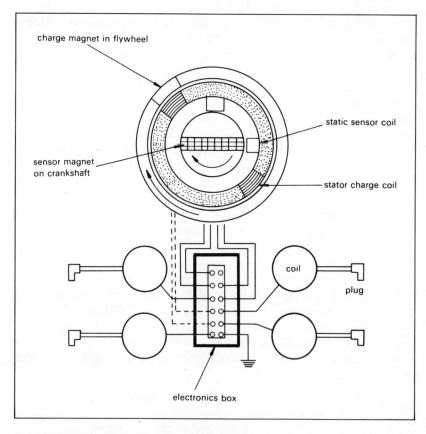

A breakerless CD ignition system. There is a coil for each plug (here, a four-cylinder engine) which means there is no need for a distributor. The rotating charge magnets acting on the static charge coil generate an AC current of several hundred volts (no battery is required). In the electronic box this is converted to DC and stored in a capacitor. When the sensor magnet passes the sensor coil, the pulse generated triggers off an electronic switch in the box (the counterpart of the contact breaker) which allows the stored current to flow through the appropriate coil. The voltage is multiplied many times in the coil, and it is this high voltage which causes a spark at the plug. Some motors have, as well as separate coils for each cylinder, separate AC generators and capacitors, thus making a virtually separate ignition system for each cylinder.

than air, so at least it will not collect in the bilge like bottled gas. The battery should be held in place in a deep tray, and in a planing or sailing boat strapped or bolted in place to prevent it bouncing out of the tray.

Corrosion of the terminals can be kept at bay by a liberal

smear of petroleum jelly (Vaseline). If the acid needs topping up very frequently this is a sign of overchanging; if current is passed into the battery after it has been fully recharged, it fizzes. The fault is likely to be in the choice of battery capacity. For alternator-fitted motors, a 60–70 amp hour battery is usually recommended, which is about twice the size of a small car's battery. The large capacity recommended is not required in particular for engine starting (outboard engines are easy to turn over compared to car engines), but partly to absorb the charging current without fizzing and partly to give ample electricity for cabin lights, etc. Many motors are *not* fitted with regulators to cut down and eventually stop the charge as the battery becomes fully charged, although the nature of an alternator circuit does give some inherent self-regulation.

If a battery keeps going flat, it is either dud, not being charged, or more current is being taken out than put in. An ammeter in the circuit is a cheap and simple instrument that shows just what is happening. It is well worth having as a permanent accessory if the motor is more or less a fixture on the boat. The only way to check on the actual state of charge is with a hydrometer. This even cheaper instrument measures the specific gravity of the acid, which varies according to the state of charge.

SG	state of charge
1.28	100%
1.25	75%
1.22	50%
1.19	25%
1.13	0%

The hydrometer reading should be corrected if the temperature is not 80°F (27°C): subtract 0.004° for each 10°F (5°C) below 27°C, and add the same amount above 27°C.

Charging systems Increasingly, modern practice is to have an alternator in the flywheel which produces AC current, and a rectifier which converts this to DC which is then fed straight to the battery. The alternator merely consists of a stator under the flywheel and magnets in the flywheel rim.

If the battery is not being charged (as shown by an ammeter), the rectifier can be checked simply with a torch battery and bulb. Disconnect the three wires and test for continuity across each of the four diodes. Diodes allow current to flow one way but not the other; consequently, for each of the four diodes the lamp should light up with the wires from the test battery and bulb one way round but not the other. Burned-out rectifiers are often discolored, having a baked appearance. The alternator stator can only be checked with an ohmmeter, the

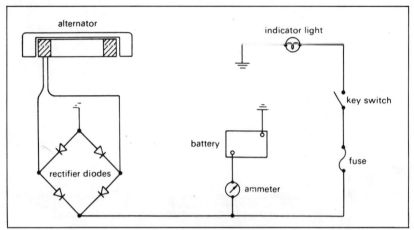

Simple alternator charging circuit.

measured values of resistance being compared to those in the workshop manual. Otherwise check for loose connections and chafed wires. Individual leads can be checked for continuity and grounding with a test battery and bulb. Whenever working on the electrics, always disconnect the battery. Wires are usually color-coded.

Some older models use a belt-driven DC generator with similar circuitry to DC generators on cars. Some Chrysler motors use a combination starter/generator mounted above the flywheel, which acts as an electric motor to start the engine and once running acts as an alternator, generating AC current, which is rectified to DC and fed into the battery.

Starter motors   Usually the starter motor is similar in writing and construction to that on a car engine, and is mounted accessibly, driving a gear ring on the flywheel. It draws a very high current from the battery via thick cables. A solenoid allows a remote starting key switch without the necessity of routing these heavy cables all the way to the switch and back. The solenoid is simply a relay; a small current from the key switch creates a strong magnetic field inside the solenoid which attracts a plunger, causing it to bridge two contacts completing the heavy current circuit to the starter motor. One can usually hear it click into place.

The starter motor itself is easy to dismantle. It is unlikely to go wrong: if it does not crank the engine over, suspect every-

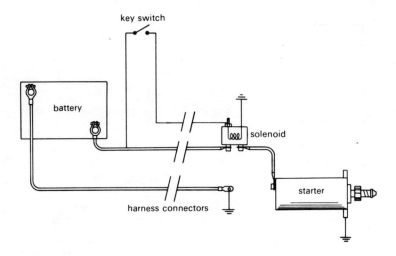

If the engine doesn't turn over, the problem is here, in the starter circuit.

thing else but the motor. The most likely reason is poor battery connections. If the starter motor is faulty, the trouble will probably lie in the brushes and commutator; worn brushes can be replaced and the commutator cleaned up. Make sure the gear pinion slides freely and snaps back to the disengaged position: a couple of drops of oil helps.

The cooling system

Water pump Overheating is likely to be caused by a worn water pump impeller or pump housing, if the water inlet grid in the lower unit is clear. A pump's life is very much dictated by the amount of grit and sand in the water in which the motor works, and if it fails after only a season or two it may be worth fitting a more wear-resistant chromium pump housing.

Separating the leg from the lower gearcase unit and repairing the water pump is probably on the borderline of the average boat owner's capability. Before embarking on the job, a workshop manual *must* be obtained, and a special tool may be required for the seals. Re-assembly is tricky involving in many

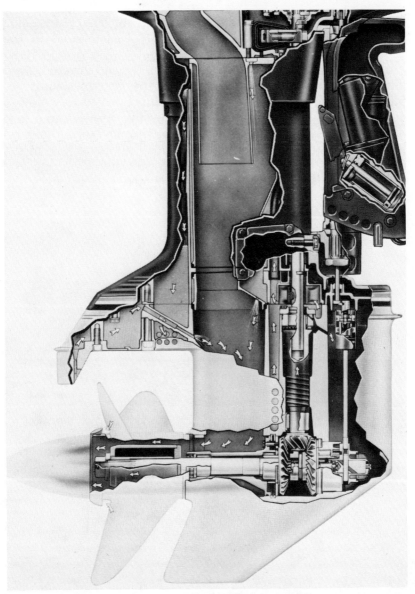

When running in water full of particulate, the cooling system will suffer from the abrasion. Check the engine regularly for overheating.

motors tightening bolts to certain torque figures and applying special sealing compounds or adhesives (partly to prevent bolts seizing through corrosion). On Mercury motors there must be no play between the drive shaft bearing and the water pump

167

base, and this entails shimming, allowing for the compression of a gasket. Precise information is only to be found in the maker's workshop manual.

The gear housing is unbolted from the leg and lowered down until the drive shaft, water pipe and the gearshift shaft are fully extracted. The pump housing is thus open to view on top of the gearcase. The interior of the housing, impeller and face plate should be inspected for wear, pitting or scoring and replaced accordingly. There may be a small air bleed hole in the plate which should be clear (e.g. Johnson and Evinrude motors). While the leg is opened up it is advisable to check the

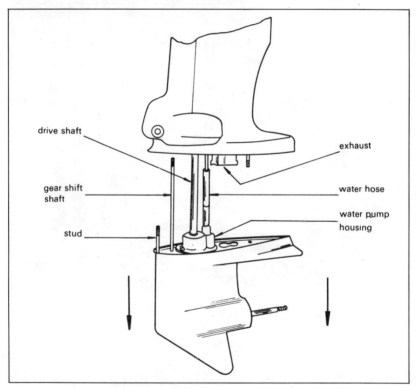

Lowering the gearcase to gain access to the water pump.

seals and bearings adjacent to the water pump and replace them if at all doubtful. Smear seals with oil to avoid damaging the surface of the rubber when fitting them. Clean the water passages to the pump face plate. When replacing the housing over the impeller turn the drive shaft in a clockwise direction so that the impeller vanes slip into the housing bent in the correct direction. The leg and gearcase are then brought together, making sure the drive shaft slips on to the splines (by slowly rotating the crankshaft) and that the water pipe emerges where it should. Overtightening the bolts may lead to stripped threads: bear in mind that aluminum is a relatively soft metal.

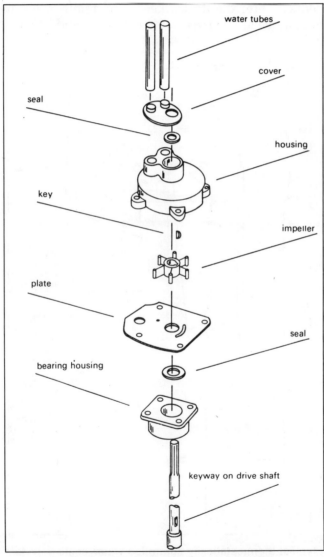

Exploded view of water pump installation.

Since water pumps are one of the parts that *do* wear, it is a pity that manufacturers don't make them more accessible by mounting them on the powerhead, perhaps with a belt drive. The unit would get maintained, and replacing the impeller while afloat would be a simple matter.

Thermostat   An engine not fitted with a thermostat runs cold at lower revs, resulting in poorer combustion and fuel economy and a reduced life; the device keeps the temperature more or less constant, usually between 100°F (38°C) and 140°F (60°C)

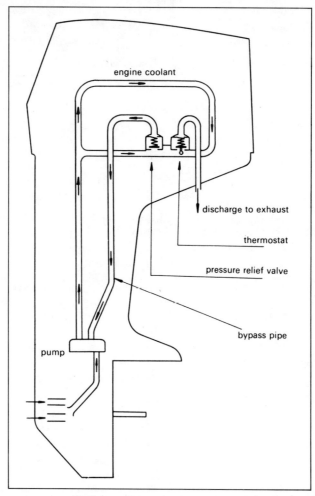

A typical thermostatically controlled water cooling system.

whatever the engine speed and water temperature. It is usually mounted very accessibly on top of the block above the spark-plug(s), so there is no great difficulty in testing or changing it if it is suspected of causing trouble. A valve in the circuit allows water to flow in a closed loop around the engine when it is first started and the thermostat is shut, shortening warm-up time; it may be integral with the thermostat or in the water pump. The valve can stick shut or open, and so can the thermostat, resulting in either cold running or overheating. One can check the valve for easy movement, and also put the thermostat in a saucepan of water and test it by heating it up. It should open well before the water boils—in fact at the specified running temperatures (above)—and the water can be tested with a kitchen thermometer. Heat-sensitive "crayons" can also be used to check the engine's correct operating temperature. With the engine running and warmed up, these heat sticks are used to mark the cylinder block or head. The marks melt at specific temperatures, and with several different sticks one can check that the cylinder temperature is within desired limits (usually the same temperature as the water should be).

Decarbonizing

If the correct fuel/oil mixture is fed to the modern outboard motor there is little need to ever decoke cylinder heads and pistons unless absolutely peak performance is required. The number of running hours clocked up by pleasure boats is quite small, though if a motor is used day in, day out on a working boat it is a different matter.

Decarbonizing a two-stroke motor is relatively easy as there is no valve block to bother with as on a four-stroke. The head is merely a cover plate over the cylinders; sometimes there are separate heads for each cylinder, sometimes a combined head. The only problem is that with some motors the engine has to be lifted to allow the head to be withdrawn off the studs without fouling the engine tray. Although not difficult, it makes the job twice as long.

Thick carbon on the piston crown and cylinder head and around the exhaust ports seriously affect performance. It should be scraped off using a blunt instrument, making sure that bits of carbon do not fall into the water passages. While the head is off, examine the cylinder walls for scoring. In refitting the cylinder head, use a new gasket and gasket sealing compound and ensure that the faces of the cylinder and cylinder head are clean and flat. Tighten the bolts in the sequence given in the workshop manual in several stages up to the correct torque. Don't tighten each bolt fully in one go or the head may be distorted: a torque wrench is vital for this job. After an hour's running the bolts should be re-torqued to the correct torque figure, thus taking up the slight initial flattening of the gasket.

The motor may be running poorly because of lack of compression in one or more cylinders, possibly caused by sticking

Carbon deposits of this magnitude on the piston crown will diminish an outboard engine's performance. Scrape the carbon off with a blunt instrument.

piston rings or just plain wear. Part of the piston rings can be inspected through the exhaust ports after taking off the exhaust cover. If they are gummed up it is worth trying an engine cleaner in the manufacturer's accessories list. It is sprayed into the carburetor while the engine is running. A compression test will quickly show whether the compression is all right or not. A pressure gauge is screwed into the sparkplug hole and the engine turned over with the starter. It is as important as the actual pressure recorded that all the cylinders should have equal pressure within about 10 psi (0.7 kg/cm²).

Four-stroke motors

In terms of maintenance, the main differences from two-strokes involve the oil in the crankcase sump or oil reservoir, and the valve gear.

The specified oil may be a straight mineral oil or a multi-grade light car engine oil. The frequency of oil changes will also be specified, and in practice this will probably turn out as a change at the end of the season and one in midseason, for average pleasure use.

There will be a sump drain plug and an oil filler, and a dipstick; the engine runs on neat gasoline. Unlike most car engines, an oil filter is not usually provided. The valve gear may be side valve, overhead camshaft (e.g. $7\frac{1}{2}$ hp Honda), or overhead valve, but the tappet adjustment will only need to be checked very infrequently. At 100 hours' running time per year, the valves should not require attention for three or four years.

Diesel outboards

As with four-stroke motors, there is an oil sump to drain and refill: diesels require special lubricating oil. A vital aspect of the diesel is the cleanliness of the fuel. Dirt will soon wreck the fuel pump and injectors, and apart from ensuring that the fuel you take aboard is clean (i.e. free of sediment and dissolved impurities), there is a filter in the line which must be cleaned regularly. If air gets into the fuel line, through leaks, loose connections, after working on the system, or from running dry, the engine will stop and the fuel system will have to be bled before it will run. The air can be got rid of by slackening an injection union and pumping fuel through with the hand lever on the engine until air-free fuel flows out.

Spares and tool kits

Inboard engine manufacturers often offer as an extra a spares or breakdown kit comprising items which are most likely to be wanted and a tool kit for individual engines. It saves a lot of shopping around for the necessary bits and pieces, and you know that the tools will fit. As far as I know, such kits are not available for outboards, but your dealer will undoubtedly advise you of the spares and tools which, in his opinion and local experience, are realistic to carry for emergency use. It is a good thing to carry them on board permanently provided they are kept dry. A toolbox with a tight lid, and lined with rust-inhibiting paper, is ideal.

If you intend to do your own outboard maintenance, it is worth getting the special tools for your particular motor—for instance a flywheel puller and hose attachment for flushing—as well as such standard tools as feeler gauges and a grease gun. It would be very helpful if outboard manufacturers also offered a simple maintenance kit including tools, spares and lubricants.

This is a basic emergency repair kit, with lubricant, sparkplug and wrench, prop nut, assorted shear and cotter pins. Keep one on board and supplement with fuel filters, wiring, and a complete set of tools.

Weights and Measures

Equivalents

Linear
1 ft. = 0.305 m = 30.5 cm = 305 mm (approx 300 mm or 30 cm)
1 in. = 2.54 cm = 25.4 mm
1 m = 100 cm = 1000 mm = 3.28 ft. = 39.4 in. (approx 40 in.)
approximate equivalents $\frac{1}{8}$ in.: 3 mm $\frac{3}{8}$in.: 10 mm $\frac{1}{2}$ in.: 13 mm

Distance
1 nautical mile (n.m.) = 6080 ft. = 1.15 statute (land) miles = 1.85 km
1 statute (land) mile = 5280 ft. = 0.87 n.m. = 1.61 km
1 km = 1000 m = 0.54 n.m. = 0.62 statute mile

Speed
1 knot = 1 n.m. per hour = 1.85 km/hr = 1.15 mph (statute miles)
1 km/hr = 0.54 knot = 0.62 mph (statute mile)
1 mph (statute mile) = 0.87 knot = 1.61 km/hr

Volume
Where "gallon" or "pint" is used in this book, the U.S. measure is meant.
1 gallon = 8 pints = 0.83 Imp gallons = 3.78 L = 0.13 cu. ft.
1 pint = 0.47 L = 470 cc
1 L = 0.26 gallon
1 L = 100 cc = 1000 ml

Fuel consumption
Fuel mileage means the distance covered on a certain quantity of fuel. In this book, mpg is always meant as *nautical* miles per U.S. gallon.

Weight
1 kg = 2.205 lb.
1 lb. = 0.454 kg
Gasoline weighs about 6–6.25 lb. per gallon (0.72–0.75 kg/L)
1 ton = 2000 lb. = 0.893 long tons = 0.907 metric tons
1 metric ton = 1000 kg = 1m³ of fresh water = 2205 lb.

Power
1 kilowatt (kW) = 1000 Watts (W)
1 hp = 1.0139 metric hp (CV) = 746 W = 550 ft. lb./sec.
watts = volts × amps

Pressure
1 atmosphere (atm) = approx 14.5 psi = 1000 mbar = 29.5 in Hg
1 psi = 0.070 kg/cm²

Appendix I
Gremlins Which Guzzle
Your Gas

It is hardly news that a well-tuned boat is critical to top performance and economy. But when it comes to actually scheduling a tune-up or replacing a damaged prop, all too many boat-owners are apt to wait until performance declines noticeably. Their procrastination can be costly.

To discover how much so, I recently traveled to Mercury Marine's famous Florida test center, Lake X. Our test boat was a brand new Sea Ray 240. With its deep-V hull, the Sea Ray is representative of the mainstream of popular mid-sized family weekenders. *Our findings apply to any gas-powered boat.*

The power plant was a 1978 MerCruiser 260 stern-drive. The engine develops 260 hp at 4,600 rpm from a 350-cu.-in. block V-8.

For our tests, the stern-drive had been replaced with a special state-of-the-art instrumented drive unit recently developed by MerCruiser. I can't say more because I was sworn to secrecy as a condition of the test. By using it, however, we were able to record on special graph paper continuous readings of rpm, boat speed, horsepower, torque and fuel consumption. No matter the horsepower, an engine that is incorrectly propped will not perform. Yet misinformation about prop selection is widespread.

The most common mistake is to pick a prop that delivers maximum engine rpm. In our Sea Ray test boat that method indicated a 17-pitch aluminum prop. Top speed was 44 mph at 4,780 rpm.

The enormous strength of stainless steel allows stainless props to have thinner blades which increase prop efficiency and reduce fuel costs.

Switching to a 19-pitch aluminum prop inched the speed up to 44.1 while the rpm dropped to 4,560. With a 19-pitch stainless steel prop, however, rpm dropped marginally to 4,520 but top speed rose to 45 mph. This is a result of the thinner blade profile possible with stainless steel which reduces drag through the water.

Finally we bolted on a 21-pitch aluminum prop. Boat speed dropped to 43.9 mph at 3,970 rpm.

Prop selection is equally important for maximum acceleration —a vital concern of water skiers and tournament fishermen. The 17-pitch aluminum prop pushed the Sea Ray to 20 mph from a standing start in 5 seconds. With both 19-pitch props the acceleration time was 6.1 seconds. The reason the stainless steel prop did not produce quicker acceleration, explained Mer-Cruiser engineer Gerald Neisen, is that at lower speeds its savings in drag is not significant.

Again the 21-pitch aluminum prop produced the slowest time —a run of 7.5 seconds.

Trim for speed

Next on our agenda was a series of test runs to determine the effect, if any, of trim angle on top speed. The results were surprising. With the stainless steel prop and the drive unit trimmed under, boat speed dropped to 41.6 mph at 4,420 rpm— a whopping loss of 8 percent in top speed.

Proper trim clearly pays a handsome dividend in performance. Unfortunately, the inaccuracy of many tachometers precludes precise trimming. Nor can you trust your ear, as I found out. As a result, anyone interested in optimizing his own boat's performance should make a series of timed runs between fixed marks. Then note the setting of the trim angle indicator on the fastest run.

The costly ding

To find out whether a damaged prop is worth replacing, we mounted a 19-pitch aluminum wheel that had been run through a sandbar. Superficially the damage was slight, consisting of one small nick out of each blade. Careful examination, however,

Depth of the prop is vitally important: too deep and drag becomes substantial; too shallow and the prop will easily ventilate, ruining performance.

A damaged prop reduces performance partially because of its greater tendency to cavitate. Cavitaion eventually causes pits and scars in the blade faces. Hence, using a damaged prop very much runs the risk of ruining it beyond repair.

revealed that the blade angle had been altered ever so slightly.

The damage proved significant as one look at the performance box will reveal. Top speed fell to 38.8 mph. Thanks to tip-induced cavitation engine speed actually rose by 150 rpm, which would mislead many skippers into thinking their boats had never run better. In fact the acceleration was off 38 percent. But most important was the 21 percent drop in optimum cruise miles per gallon.

The lesson is clear. Forget all that advice about dressing a damaged blade with a file and repainting. Replace any damaged prop. The fuel savings will pay for it in a typical season.

Ignition timing

Everyone knows that ignition timing is important to engine performance. But few realize that it is as critical as our tests revealed.

With the timing set to 6° after top dead center (instead of 8° before TDC) the engine started easily, idled and ran smoothly. Even more misleading, top speed dropped by only 1.5 mph, which would be undetected by a speedometer. Acceleration was off by a surprising 41 percent, however.

But the biggest surprise was the effect on fuel economy. At optimum cruise, the instruments revealed a mammoth 39 percent drop in miles per gallon from our base line of 3.3 mpg.

Any engine can go out of time from routine operation because of wear in the points breaker block. Also an engine should be carefully timed after replacing ignition points. As the tests proved, a periodic tune-up is money well spent.

Shorted spark plug

To simulate the effect of a severely fouled spark plug, we removed one of the ignition wires. Again the engine started and ran easily, although there was a noticeable roughness. Nevertheless the dead cylinder clipped only 2.6 mph off the top speed. But the loss was extremely damaging to fuel economy—cruise mpg fell by 33 percent.

Carburetor bugs

The final test was to evaluate the effect of a closed secondary valve in the carburetor. In normal operation the secondary is pulled open by vacuum to increase engine power in the higher speed ranges. Corrosion and an accumulation of grease and grime can cause the valve to stick shut. When that happens boat performance suffers. Top speed fell by 4.8 mph while acceleration slowed a dramatic 37.7 percent.

Ferreting out these performance gremlins took the better part of two days. But the results were worth it. The facts speak for themselves. The next time somebody starts complaining that tune-ups are a come-on to keep marina mechanics rich, don't bother to listen. Now you know better.   —*Oliver Moore*

Appendix II
Pre-Launch Check List

For those whose rigs have remained idle during the winter months, the minutes spent in pre-launch propulsion system checks and adjustments will mean hours of trouble-free operation in the season ahead. Even where boats are used on a year-round basis, these procedures should be followed on a regular schedule to insure optimum engine performance.

Batteries

Inspect the battery for cracks or bulges in the case and signs of electrolyte leakage. Fill cells to proper level with distilled water or water passed through a "demineralizer." Be sure the top of the battery is clean—dirt and even an acid film between terminals can act as a voltage conductor. To clean: Wash with a dilute ammonia or soda solution, then flush with freshwater (making sure vent plugs are tight so the solution does not enter the cells).

Check the battery hold-downs. They should be tight enough to keep the battery from shaking around in its holder, but not so tight as to put a strain on it. Clean terminal posts and battery clamps with the soda solution, rinse and dry. Apply a thin coat of multipurpose lubricant to posts and clamps to help retard corrosion. Check the battery cables, too; replace if necessary.

Controls

Remote controls should be inspected for damage and function. Things to look for are bent push-pull rods; deformed or "bubbled" sleeves; swelling under jacket; cracked, cut or abraided jacket; or separation of the jacket at a hub. Operate controls through their entire range. The effort should be constant, with no "sticky" spots, except for the detents at forward, neutral and reverse.

If the cables are more than a few years old, or if they have been subject to rough or continuous use, your best bet is to replace them, even if operation seems smooth at this time and a visual inspection shows no defects. Adjust steering and engine control cables to eliminate slack.

Fuel system

Give special attention to your fuel system, from tank(s) to engine. If old fuel in tanks was not treated with a stabilizer, discard it (properly and safely). Refill with fresh gasoline after inspecting tank for signs of water, rust or corrosion. Clean and repaint any nicks or scrapes in the finish as the bare metal can rust rapidly. If there is any doubt as to the integrity of a tank, replace it.

If outboard tanks are not those supplied by the motor manufacturer, be sure pickups, filters and lines are large enough to

Fuel filters are easy to inspect and replace. They must be free of dust and lint, and of the size and mesh specified by the outboard maker.

provide adequate fuel flow. A restricted flow results in fuel starvation at the motor—a lean mixture not only means a loss of rpm, but possibly scored or burned pistons. If in doubt about your tanks, check with your engine dealer.

When adding fresh outboard fuel, *stick* to the oil-mix ratio specified by the motor manufacturer, and use only an oil formulated for outboard use. More or less oil in the gas may not change the lubricating quality of the mix, but the proportion of *additives* may be thrown way out of balance. Extensive engine damage may result.

Be sure all fuel filters are clean in tanks and at the engine. If there's a filter in the fuel line, replace it with a fresh one. All filters should be checked every 50 hours of engine operation, as a clogged one chokes off the fuel supply to the engine.

Inspect fuel lines for kinks, bends and leaks. On inboards, remove and clean flame arrestors, using a nonflammable solvent, then blow dry with compressed air before reinstallation. Check choke operation to make sure the butterfly valve opens and closes fully.

Spark plugs

Remove and inspect spark plugs; plug tip color is a good indicator of general engine condition. Make sure plugs are gapped to manufacturer's specs; rim fire-type outboard plugs probably will fire properly if the center electrode has not burned more than $\frac{1}{32}''$ below the rim. However, it's a good idea to start the season with fresh plugs and to carry a set of sealed spares in your toolbox. Before installing plugs, make sure their seats are clean, and use new gaskets if you're using the old plugs.

If you're getting engine-generated static on your radio-telephone, this is a good time to add the plugs, cables and condensers that will eliminate this interference. (*Your Boat's Electrical System*, by Conrad Miller, details the steps for this and presents a wealth of additional useful information. It's available from Motor Boating & Sailing Books, P.O. Box 2319, FDR Station, New York, NY 10022; price is $7.50.)

Replace plugs carefully to avoid damage to plug seat threads in the cylinder block or head. Seat each plug fingertight, then tighten an additional half-turn with a wrench. If you have a torque wrench, tighten to 20 foot pounds (2.76 mkg). Improper installation is one of the greatest single causes of unsatisfactory outboard spark plug performance, according to Mercury Marine engineers.

Inspect plug leads for abrasion, cracks or worn insulation, particularly where insulation is in contact with metal parts. High-voltage current leaking through to ground means a weak spark at the plug. Replace wiring as necessary.

Drive units

Check outboard lower units for damaged or loose parts, and make replacements or tighten as necessary. Clean the entire unit thoroughly, and apply primer and matching paint to damaged or corroded surfaces. This is an important step in the prevention of galvanic corrosion.

Top-up the unit with the recommended lubricant. This should be changed every 100 hours of operation, or at least once a season, so this is a good time to drain the old stuff and refill with new. On some small outboards, it's necessary to lay the engine on its side to drain it; don't raise the lower unit so it is higher than the powerhead, or even so that it can drain toward the powerhead. Any water in the gearcase would run into the powerhead, where it could damage bearings if not removed immediately.

Be sure filler and drain plug sealing gaskets are in place after adding the lubricant, or the grease will leak out and water will seep in. Water will seriously damage gears and bearings.

Many drive units are fitted with power options for trim angle and power steering. Check all electrical and hydraulic connections and tighten as required. Where mechanical steering cable requires lubrication, use a hand-operated grease gun, not a high-pressure type. Apply lubricant next to the hand nut where it is connected to the cable guide tube, making sure the cable is in a retracted position so a hydraulic lock doesn't occur. Also grease the exposed cable traveling through the cable guide tube, the upper and lower pivot pins of the gimbal housing, and the tilt pins on both sides of the gimbal housing, if the drive is so equipped.

Replace the anti-corrosion zinc with a fresh one, if more than 50 percent worn. Often these are in the form of the adjustable trim tabs used to counteract propeller torque.

Propellers

Remove the propeller and inspect the hub for possible damage. Whenever the propeller shaft nut is removed or installed on an outboard, place a block of wood between the wheel and the cavitation plate. The modern outboards start so easily that a spin of the propeller, with the transmission in gear, could accidentally start the motor.

Inspect the propeller itself carefully; those "minor" nicks and dents can knock several miles off a boat's top speed, cut acceleration by 25 percent or more and lower fuel efficiency by as much as 20 percent. Small nicks and burrs can be dressed with a file, taking care to remove as little metal as possible. But the best bet—especially with more extensive damage—is to have the wheel repaired by a professional or replaced by a new one.

You might consider a new wheel if performance last year was not satisfactory. Remember, the wheel that lets the engine rev up the highest doesn't always mean the most speed if the engine is past is maximum torque point. Work with the dealer to get the propeller that best suits your needs, whether top speed, cruising economy, or acceleration for water-skiers. Consider one of the strong new stainless steel wheels; the initial high cost may be a saving over the long run.

Coat the shaft splines with a good waterproof lubricant before reinstalling a propeller. This facilitates removal of the propeller later by preventing corrosion that can "freeze" the wheel to the shaft.

Outboard powerheads

Remove and clean the cowling, and all accessible powerhead parts. Retouch any damaged or scraped painted surfaces. While the spark plugs are out, remove oil deposits that form in cylinders and crankcase by operating the starter for a few moments. Use the starter rope to turn over the crankshaft on manual-start models; on all models check the starter rope for wear.

Be sure clamps on small engines, and bolts on larger ones, are tightened securely so the motor won't come adrift from the transom. When the boat is launched (make sure the drain is closed), make your running adjustments with an average load on board. The tilt pin should be set so the boat rides on an even keel, and trim tabs should be adjusted so the boat steers with equal ease in either direction. Idle and high-speed carburetor adjustments can be made on many models; but where carburetor cleaning, magneto or breaker point adjustments are needed, these should be done by a qualified dealer's mechanic.

—Tom Bottomley